Empowering Students;

Hands-on Library Instruction Activities

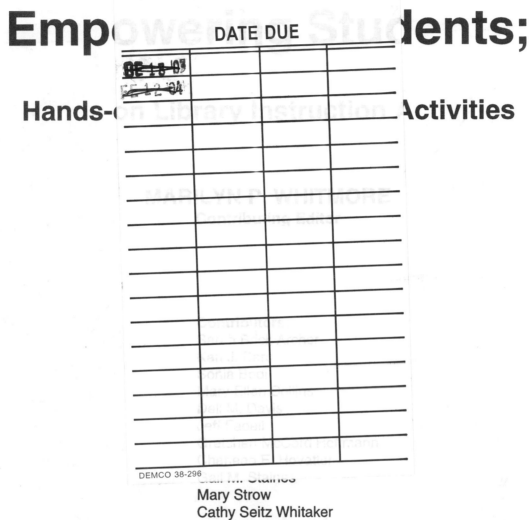

Mary Strow
Cathy Seitz Whitaker
Marilyn P. Whitmore

LIBRARY INSTRUCTION PUBLICATIONS

Library of Congress Catalog Card Number: 96-76757

ISBN: 0-9652711-0-2

Printed by Whitmore Printing & Typesetting in Lancaster, Pennsylvania

Contents

Preface

This is a librarian's book of sharing "How We Do What We Do." Librarians who are responsible for instruction spend a great deal of time teaching students about libraries, about how to find information, and about how these two go hand in hand. But how much do they remember when they walk out the door? We want what we teach students to remain with them until they come to the library the next time, or until they have to write a research paper, find a book review, a map to locate a place, the address of a congressman, or fulfill any other information need.

How can we make learning a fun experience that carries over to other times and various situations? We are told by educators that adults learn best when they are involved in active learning in their own style and at their own pace. One excellent way to help achieve real learning is to provide a structured opportunity to "experience" information seeking. Time is important to students, so we want to save them countless hours of unproductive research time.

Empowering Students; Hands-on Library Instruction Activities provides 20 basic lesson plans contributed by 12 librarians from different institutions around the United States. The lesson plans include the reasons instruction was undertaken at each author's institution, the learning objectives, the components of the in-class instruction, hands-on exercises or student activities, evaluation, and suggestions for teaching variations. Some authors have included in-depth bibliographies such as the Children's Literature Pathfinder in the chapter "Meeting the Author" by Mary Ellen Collins.

The book has been divided into four sections as indicated in the contents:

- Classroom activities for teaching basic concepts (the hands-on activities in these chapters are for in-class work)

- Activities appropriate for 2 or 3 students (the responsibility of the search process is shared by the team)

- Group activities for up to 6 students (some activities to be completed in the classroom setting and others as homework)

- Activities planned for individuals (either in-class or home work assignments)

In order for librarians to utilize this book effectively, the activity sheets can be photocopied and distributed to their students. The activities are also available on disk either for the Macintosh or for DOS machines; the software used is Microsoft WORD. The advantage of the disk is that each library can then modify the activities to fit their local situation whether this means substituting titles, adding call numbers, etc.

The content of this book will be appropriate and useful not only at the college or university level but also for junior college and upper-level high school students. The reference tools included in the student activities are basic and will be found in most libraries.

Background

Several years ago, I began the time-consuming task of developing a unique library exercise or activity for each student in a research writing class which was scheduled for six library instruction sessions. Students selected their own research topics with the approval of their classroom instructor; the topics ranged from an investigation of the pituitary gland in older horses to the influence of baseball on the American culture. Each term I developed search strategies for a wide variety of topics. Because I had committed much time and effort to this project, I was anxious to evaluate whether my instructional objectives had been achieved; not only were my objectives achieved, but both faculty and student evaluations at the end of each term were very positive.

I began doing similar exercises for other courses. For example, a newspaper writing class required that each student write an obituary, so I designed exercises using biographical reference sources. I constantly reworked the exercises and created new ones. This book is the outcome of my realization that all this hard work should be shared with colleagues with the hope that they will find practical applications for this information in their own library instruction sessions.

I want to especially thank the contributing authors for sharing their library instruction lesson plans. Without the variation they have provided, this book would not have been nearly as innovative. I also wish to express my gratitude to Dr. Rush Miller, Director of the University Library System at the University of Pittsburgh for his encouragement and support.

Librarians are urged to contact me with their suggestions for making this series of books more useful to the profession. I also encourage all those who are interested in sharing their lesson plans and active learning exercises to contact me.

Marilyn P. Whitmore
Editor, Library Instruction Publications
222 Lytton Avenue
Pittsburgh, PA 15213-1410
Voice/FAX: 412 687-1844
mpw+@pitt.edu

Meet the Contributing Authors

Sarah Brick Archer is an Assistant Professor of Library Services and serves as the Reference/Resource Coordination Librarian for the College of Arts and Letters at Northeastern State University in Tahlequah, Oklahoma. She has published an article about using teams in training and presented a paper at the 23rd Annual LOEX conference on incorporating performance techniques in library instruction. E-mail: archersa@cherokee.nsuok.edu

Kari J. Bero is a part-time reference librarian/Internet trainer at Pierce College in Lakewood, WA and is the owner of Bero-West Indexing Services in Seattle. She was previously the User Education Coordinator in the Reference and Research Services Division of the University of Washington in Seattle. E-mail: alexia.lis.uiuc.edu

Sonia Bodi is Head Reference Librarian and Professor of Bibliography at North Park College in Chicago. As a member of the faculty, she chairs the Division of Humanities, a position she has held since 1988. Sonia is the author of several published articles on library instruction. E-mail: sbodi@npcts.edu

Mary Ellen Collins is an Associate Professor of Library Science and Reference Librarian at the Purdue University Libraries. She taught in grade school before joining the library profession 26 years ago. Since then, she has taught children's literature and reference in college and university settings, along with serving in libraries. Mary Ellen has also served on committees in the ALA and state associations, and is the author of a book and several articles. Her MLS and PhD are from the University of Pittsburgh. E-mail:collinsm@sage.cc.purdue.edu

Dell M. Davis is the Social Sciences Librarian at the University of Houston. She is heavily involved in the library instruction program, teaching classes, writing reference guides, and developing and enhancing library literacy outreach programs. She is active in ALA committees and the Texas Library Association. Her MLS is from the University of North Texas.

John E. "Jeff" Fadell has been a reference librarian specializing in library instruction at the University of Houston since 1980. He has been very active in producing instructional videotapes, writing and editing library handouts and guides, and in the development of electronic reference services. Jeff received his MA and PhD from the University of Minnesota; the MLS is from the University of Texas at Austin. He may be reached by e-mail at: jef@uh.edu.

Gretchen McCord Hoffmann is Coordinator of Library Instruction at the University of Houston. Gretchen has given conference presentations on aspects of library instruction, including "Library Instruction in Transition: Questioning Current Views," to be published in the proceedings of the Finding Common Ground Conference. She was editor of "In Reference to Libraries," the library handbook from which the excerpts of her chapter in this book were taken. Gretchen holds an MSIS from the University of North Texas and a BA in sociology and psychology from Rice University. E-mail: gmhoffmann@uh.edu

Charlene E. Hovatter is Library Instruction and Reference Librarian in Hillman Library, the primary library for Social Sciences and Humanities at the University of Pittsburgh. She received a BA in Philosophy from Mount Holyoke College and an MLS from the University of Kentucky. Charlene is currently Editor of the ACRL Women's Studies Section Newsletter. She can be reached via e-mail at cehova@vms.cis.pitt.edu.

Gail M. Staines is currently Coordinator of Library Instruction at Niagara County Community College, Sanborn, NY. She holds the MLS and a PhD in Higher Education Administration from the University of Buffalo where she is also an adjunct Assistant Professor. Gail is a library instruction consultant and guest speaker and was selected to be on the first list of ACRL's Information Literacy Advisors. Gail is the author of several articles. She may be reached via e-mail at: staines@alpha.sunyniagara.cc.ny.us.

Mary Strow has been a librarian in the Undergraduate Library at Indiana University Bloomington since 1989. For six years she served as Librarian for Instructional Services and was responsible for coordinating instructional programs. She has been a presenter at LOEX and is involved in research and publishing in the area of dance. Mary is actively involved in the work of the ACRL Arts Section of the American Library Association. E-mail: mstrow@indiana.edu.

Cathy Seitz Whitaker was the Buhl Social Work Librarian at the University of Pittsburgh from 1990–1993. She authored numerous handouts for the social work students and taught all of the library instruction classes for the School of Social Work. Cathy received an MLS from the University of Illinois and an MA in Political Science from Miami University, Miami, OH. She presently lives in Toledo. and may be consulted at: cwhitaker@aol.com.

Marilyn P. Whitmore is Editor of Library Instruction Publications and former Coordinator of Library Instruction in the University of Pittsburgh Libraries, 1984–1995. She has been active in ALA, especially the units dealing with instruction, collections development, and international library issues. Marilyn is the author of numerous publications. She holds the MLS from Rutgers University and PhD from the University of Pittsburgh. Contact by E-mail is: mpw+@pitt.edu.

CLASSROOM ACTIVITIES FOR TEACHING BASIC CONCEPTS

This section contains:

Scholarly Journals vs Popular Magazines
Gail M. Staines

Propaganda or Scholarship: How to Tell the Difference
Sonia Bodi

Critical Thinking and the Search Strategy Approach in an Education Class
Sonia Bodi

Basic Tools and Unique Strategies in a Speech Communications Class
Kari J. Bero

Examining Reference Sources
Gail M. Staines

NOTES:

Scholarly Journals vs. Popular Magazines

GAIL M. STAINES

Coordinator of Library Instruction
NIAGARA COUNTY COMMUNITY COLLEGE, SANBORN, NY

Circumstances for the Instruction Session:

Understanding the differences between scholarly articles and articles published in popular magazines can be a new concept to first and second year undergraduate students. This is an important distinction for students to be able to identify, especially for those students at the community college level who are planning on transferring to a four-year college or university.

One of the easiest ways to introduce students to the differences is to have them explore the publications in an interactive environment. The exercise outlined below can be integrated into any library instruction session where identifying scholarly material is important.

Goal: Students at Niagara County Community College are able to identify scholarly journals and popular magazines.

Objectives of the Instruction:

Upon completion of this library instruction session:

- Students use the research strategy concept to locate information on their topic.
- Students are able to list differences between scholarly journal articles and popular magazine articles.
- Students are able to identify a citation to a scholarly journal article using an index on CD-ROM. eg., *The Social Sciences Index* on CD-ROM.

Components of the Library Instruction:

Various classes in different disciplines across the curriculum require students to complete a research paper or give an oral presentation citing scholarly sources. Such courses include, but are not limited to, Introduction to Human Services, Human Services Research and Synthesis, Community Studies, Introduction to Sociology, Abnormal Psychology, etc. Students must cite scholarly literature and may not use articles from popular magazines such as *Time* or *Newsweek*. Development of the paper and reference list follows *APA* format.

This interactive library instruction session works best in a 75-minute time period, although it can be completed in 50 minutes. The session is divided into three parts.

Part 1   Introduction (10–15 minutes)

The first 10–15 minutes of this session provides background information to the students. During this time:

- the librarian and faculty member review expectations of the research paper or oral presentation;

- the librarian explains a research strategy for locating relevant information;

- students are asked if there are any questions about their assignment (this occurs throughout the session).

Part 2   Hands-on Activity (15 minutes)

Students are separated into groups of no more than 6 students per group. The librarian asks the students to select one student in each group to take notes and another student to be a spokesperson for the group.

Each group receives two copies of a scholarly journal and two copies of a popular magazine. (Copies are weeded issues of periodicals.) Examples of scholarly journals which have been used are *AJN*, *JAMA*, and *American Journal of Sociology*. Examples of popular magazines which have been used are *Newsweek*, *Time*, and *Changing Times*. During the 5–7 minutes of comparing, the librarian and faculty member check with each group to determine the progress and answer any questions.

After comparisons have been completed, each group spokesperson reports on **one difference** between the popular magazine and scholarly journal. Each group tries to report on unique differences from the previous group.

At the end of this activity, the librarian reviews the differences between the scholarly journal and magazine article with a handout and a transparency and/or presentation slides using software such as PowerPoint or Harvard Graphics. A sample list of differences which can be used for projection is attached.

Part 3   Identifying a Scholarly Journal on CD-ROM

After students identify differences between the scholarly and popular literature, the librarian teaches students how to search a CD-ROM index for a scholarly article. Students are asked to suggest a topic to search. The librarian demonstrates the search on the CD-ROM index using a computer, CD-ROM player, LCD panel, and overhead projector. When a citation is found, the librarian asks the students if the citation is scholarly. Students look for identifying characteristics of a scholarly journal such as inclusion of a bibliography and page length.

At the end of the session, the librarian reviews the research strategy, the characteristics of scholarly and popular literature, and searching a CD-ROM index for an article. The librarian and faculty member ask students if there are any more questions. If time permits, students are taken to the area of the library where the indexes are located to get started on their research. The librarian and faculty member are available to answer questions.

Evaluation:

Evaluation of this library instruction session is informal. Students receive a survey of library instruction several weeks after the library instruction session. The students are asked for their reactions to the instruction and their perceptions concerning the librarian's preparedness for teaching. Student feedback as well as observation show that students are able to identify scholarly journal articles.

SCHOLARLY JOURNALS VS. POPULAR MAGAZINES*

SCHOLARLY JOURNALS	POPULAR MAGAZINES
Bibliographies or references included	Usually DO NOT have bibliographies or references
Authors are experts	Authors are often generalists
Articles are signed by the authors	Articles are sometimes unsigned
Audience is the scholarly reader, such as professors, researchers, students	Audience is the general population
Standardized formats are usually followed like *APA, MLA,* etc.	Various formats which are often unstructured
Written in the jargon of the field	Written for anyone to understand
Any illustrations support the text, such as maps, tables, photographs	Often profusely illustrated for marketing appeal

*This handout was modified from a handout created by the University of Michigan, and from a figure published in Cook, Kim N., Lilith R. Kunkel, and Susan M. Weaver. "Cooperative Learning in Bibliographic Instruction." *Research Strategies* Winter 1995 :17–25.

Propaganda or Scholarship: How to Tell the Difference

SONIA BODI

Professor of Bibliography
NORTH PARK COLLEGE & SEMINARY, CHICAGO

Circumstances of the Instruction Session:

Helping students understand the differences between propaganda and scholarship can be included in every instructional session librarians present. We sometimes give students a handout of the indicators of propaganda and scholarship (see next page), and we always encourage students to be skeptical of information. We help them understand that information is not knowledge until the students engage their own analysis, synthesis and evaluation. A sample list of differences which can be projected on a screen is attached.

This particular instruction is primarily for first-year students as part of their English composition class. First-year students are enrolled in one semester of English composition which is a two-part course. The first half of the course focuses on general writing skills at the college level and includes first-year library instruction. The second half of the course focuses on writing within the context of a particular topic.

One of the English professors usually chooses propaganda as the topic for the second part of his English composition course. The students read John Dower's *War Without Mercy* (New York: Pantheon, 1987) which is a splendid example of a well-balanced work of scholarship examining the use of propaganda by both the Americans and the Japanese during World War II. This library instruction is done in a 70-minute class period.

Objectives of the Instruction:

Students will begin to understand the differences between scholarship based on careful and fair-minded research and scholarship based on disinformation and propaganda.

Components of the Library Instruction:

Twenty different articles were compiled from the bibliography of *War Without Mercy*; some of the articles are examples of propaganda and some are examples of scholarship. All of the students read one article in common, Virginius Dabney, "Nearer and Nearer the Precipice." *Atlantic Monthly* (January 1943): 94–100, and all read their individual article as well.

The articles are distributed for students to read prior to the library presentation. The presentation begins with a brief lecture on propaganda and on some of the differences between propaganda and scholarship. We emphasize the following indicators:

Indicators of Scholarship

- Describes limits of data

- Presents accurate description of alternative views

- Presents data that do not favor preferred views as well as data that support these

- Encourages debate/discussion/criticism

- Settles disputes by use of generally accepted criteria for evaluating data

- Looks for counter-examples

- Uses language in agreed-on ways

- Updates information.

- Admits own ignorance

- Attempts to discuss general laws/principles

- Finds own field/area of investigation difficult and full of holes

- Relies on critical thinking skills

Indicators of Propaganda

- Excessive claims of certainty. (We have "the way;" "the view")

- Personal attacks/ridicule

- Emotional appeals

- Distortions of data unfavorable to preferred views

- Suppresses contradictory views

- Suppresses contradictory facts

- Appeals to popular prejudices

- Relies on suggestion (e.g., negative innuendo)

- Devalues thought/critical appraisal

- Transforms words to suit aims

- Magnifies or minimizes problems/suggested remedies

- Presents information/views out of context

We then discuss the article, "Nearer and Nearer the Precipice," which was read in common. Students will read this article from a contemporary viewpoint and will judge the article to be racist. This is a good opportunity to talk about reading primary sources from the viewpoint of its time of writing. After the discussion, students will have a different understanding of the article.

Each student has been assigned an article to read ahead of time. At this point, the class is divided into groups of four which are determined by the common subject matter of their articles. For example, one group of articles covers the psychology of the war, another the actual fighting, another the issue of color, and another the Japanese perspective. After discussing the articles using the Indicators listed on the preceding page, each group selects a spokesperson to summarize the findings to the entire class. The articles are from news magazines, scholarly journals and popular magazines of the time.

After these presentations, the professor of the course has the students work in groups of four to research and produce a 10-page literature review on one aspect of propaganda. The students choose topics such as "The media in the Vietnam War: what effects did the media have on the peace movement at home?;" "Propaganda and racism: how much does propaganda depend on racial prejudice for its success?;" and "The process of defining an enemy: what common characteristics do enemies have?"

After working collaboratively on a group research project, the students each take one aspect of their group project such as "Race in the propaganda films of Frank Capra: how much was the films' motivation to fight based on racial stereotypes of the Japanese?" and "Propaganda and the nightly news: does the nightly news portray crime in racist terms?" Students write a fifteen page research paper as their final assignment for the course.

Evaluation:

In their written evaluation of the instruction which was done at the end of the course, a few students said they had not thought about propaganda before and the instruction helped them better understand what it is. Others thought they already understood what propaganda is but as a result of the instruction they realized they had much to learn. The rest of the class seemed to have no opinion.

The professor, in his assessment, said that the students fell into another error. That is, if a scholar had a dissenting voice on an issue, the students thought it was not propaganda but an honest critique. Students also may confuse the delivery with the information conveyed and think a flawed delivery means propaganda and a well-constructed delivery means scholarship.

This assignment is one step of many in the process of helping students critically assess the scholarly merit and relevance of the sources they find and use. Many of these small steps need to be part of their undergraduate experience. Giving students a brief lecture on propaganda and scholarship can be part of the instruction in a variety of classes.

Bibliography of Articles Used:

"Jap Surrenders are Increasing: Psychological War Proves Effective." *Life* 19(July 9, 1945).

Edgar Jones, "Fighting with Words: Psychological Warfare in the Pacific." *Atlantic Monthly* 76(Aug 1945): 47–51.

Karl Lowith, "The Japanese Mind: A Picture of the Mentality That We Must Understand if We Are to Conquer." *Fortune* 27(December 1943): 132–135.

Judith Silberpfenning, "Psychological Aspects of Current Japanese and German Paradoxa." *Psychoanalytical Review* 32(January 1945): 73–85.

"Murder in Tokyo." *Time* 41 (May 3, 1943): 19–20.

"How Japs Fight." *Time* 41(February 15, 1943):24–26.

"Bataan: Where Heroes Fell." *Time* 40(April 20, 1942): 18–21.

"The Jap as Boss-Man." *Time* 41 (May 3, 1943): 26.

"Why Americans Hate Japs More Than Nazis." *Science Digest* 17 (March 1945): 5.

Charles Bolte, "This is the Face of War." *The Nation* 160(March 3, 1945): 240–241.

Helen Mears, "Why the Japanese Fight." *The New Republic* 108(March 29, 1943): 418–419.

Roger Bastide, "Color, Racism and Christianity." *Daedelus* 96(Spring 1967): 312–327.

"Are We Afraid to Do Justice?" *Christian Century* 60(June 9, 1943): 687–688.

Hiroshi Wagatsuma, "The Social Perception of Skin Color in Japan." *Daedelus* 96(Spring 1967): 407–443.

Kodansha Encyclopedia, s.v . "Foreigners, Attitudes Toward."

John Embree, "Democracy in Postwar Japan." *American Journal of Sociology* 50 (November 1944): 205–207.

Joel Berreman, "Assumptions About America in Japanese War Propaganda to the United States." *American Journal of Sociology* 54(September 1948): 108–117.

Kodansha Encyclopedia, s.v. "World War II."

This instructional session is from:
Sonia Bodi, "Scholarship or Propaganda: How Can Librarians Help Undergraduates Tell the Difference?" *The Journal of Academic Librarianship* 21 (January 1995): 21–26.

DIFFERENCES BETWEEN PROPAGANDA AND SCHOLARSHIP

PROPAGANDA	SCHOLARSHIP
Operates with many levels of both truth and falsehood	Strives for truth and admits weaknesses
Presents one point of view as the only point of view	Presents other points of view and may include dissenting points of view
Misleads deliberately	Attempts to be fair-minded and admits bias or viewpoint
Manipulates charts, graphs, statistics to support a premise	Interprets data carefully whether they support or refute a premise
Provides ready-made answers and solutions to problems	Invites critical analysis
Results in changed attitude and/or motivation to action to be successful	Invites continuing research

NOTES:

Critical Thinking and the Search Strategy Approach in an Education Class

SONIA BODI

Professor of Bibliography
NORTH PARK COLLEGE & SEMINARY, CHICAGO

Circumstances of the Instruction Session:

Professors attempt to teach students to examine texts and issues in a critical manner, to question assumptions, to recognize when it is necessary to question, and to carry out evaluations and analyses in a rational manner. Further, an important component of any instructional session is critical thinking and the evaluation of information. Education is one of the disciplines in which issues have a multiplicity of viewpoints and no easy answers. The following instruction is presented to a class in education in which we focus on reinforcing critical thinking skills.

The course, Development of Educational Thought, taken by third-year students, presents the development of educational thought through a study of different educational philosophies, institutions, and laws. The class enrollment of 25 to 30 students includes students whose majors are in elementary education, physical education, music, English, math, biology, art, and foreign language. Halfway through the term, after the students have gained some background and have been assigned a 10-item annotated bibliography on an educational issue of their choice, we present the instruction. This is a 70-minute class.

Objectives of the Instruction:

- To help students understand there is a multiplicity of points of view in education each of which must be examined carefully.

- To help prospective teachers learn to think critically so they in turn can teach their students to think critically.

Components of the Library Instruction:

The instruction consists of two parts: a debate and a demonstration of a search strategy.

Part 1 The Debate:

In preparing for the debate, the professor and the librarian discuss current "hot" issues in education that might serve as material for a debate between the two of them. These issues are so numerous that the problem becomes one of narrowing the choice to the one that would be most interesting to argue in class with the students. For example, with elementary education and English majors it is interesting to debate the philosophy of Whole Language. Inclusion of multicultural studies is an issue of interest to all of the students.

Whatever the issue, a debate between the professor and the librarian readily draws students into the post-debate discussion, during which the professor also presents and asks for student opinions on other controversial issues. In arguing the cases, the librarian and the professor try to use concrete examples and avoid defending a position on purely emotional grounds—techniques that demonstrate a critical approach to studying an issue.

Part 2 Demonstration of Search Strategy:

After the 35-minute debate and discussion, we spend the next 35 minutes demonstrating how a search strategy can help students to look more critically at the issues involved in their annotated bibliography assignment. The students are already familiar with this approach through their first-year library instruction and other course-related bibliographic instruction classes. We usually are aware of some of the topics already chosen by students and can refer to these topics while going through the search strategy.

The search strategy begins with the *Encyclopedia of Educational Research*. We bring to the class all of the sources we discuss and pass them around for students to become familiar with them. The *Encyclopedia of Educational Research* summarizes the different perspectives on a wide range of educational issues giving students a concise background on the issues. Each article is followed by a bibliography which we always encourage students to consult.

We next encourage students to look at the qualifications of the author. Not only will they have some idea of the author's authority to write on the topic, but they will also discover the author's perspective. Students need to know there is a difference between someone writing from practical experience as a teacher of children and adolescents, and someone writing from a theoretical base as a college or university professor.

At this point we also remind students of the *Book Review Digest* and the *Book Review Index*. Reading reviews written by scholars in the field is important in their evaluation of the source.

We introduce students to *ERIC* on CD-ROM for journal literature and explain the differences between scholarly journals such as *Harvard Educational Review* and practical journals such as *English Journal.* We display Katz's *Magazines for Libraries* as a way of helping students judge the audience and perspective of the journal.

Other sources are introduced, although not all will be used by all of the students. Depending on their topic, students may use legal and statistical sources such as *Deskbook Encyclopedia of American School Law, The Condition of Education, Digest of Educational Statistics,* and *Projections of Education Statistics.*

Finally, we help them locate subjects in the on-line catalog. Our goal, however, is for the students to depend on bibliographies they find and then look for books by title, rather than to look for subjects headings haphazardly.

Requirements for the annotated bibliography include information about the author, the purpose of the book or journal article, the intended audience, author bias, the author's methodology, conclusions, and relationship to other works included in the bibliography. Students also look carefully at the author's bibliography and assess its relevance and significance.

Evaluation:

Students seem to be aware that there are few easy answers in education. Issues are complex and multifaceted and they learn that they need to search a variety of sources for a balanced view. The session demonstrates that critical thinking requires one to look carefully at the different sides of an issue before determining which position is the most tenable. Perhaps the approach has contributed in some measure to educating prospective teachers to think critically, thus enabling this skill to be passed on to the next generation of students.

This instructional session is from:
Sonia Bodi, "Critical Thinking and Bibliographic Instruction: The Relationship." *The Journal of Academic Librarianship* 14 (July 1988): 150–153.

NOTES:

Basic Tools and Unique Strategies in a Speech Communications Class

Kari J. Bero

Indexer
Bero-West Indexing Services, Seattle, WA

Circumstances for the Instruction:

This innovative library assignment was created for a Speech Communications, Introduction to Public Speaking class at the University of Washington (UW). One of the course goals is for students to learn "choice and organization" of information in reference tools in preparation for informative and persuasive speeches.

Instructors noticed that the information students heard in library sessions wasn't retained. Students were still having trouble comprehending differences between similar kinds of reference tools, understanding how information in those tools is organized, and learning how to effectively retrieve information from them.

In this unique assignment, **student do hands-on exercises before their library session**. The idea behind this was that students would be more willing to listen and more likely to remember librarians' advice if they see where they could have applied the strategies to save them time. In other words, since students seem to learn more the hard way, why not use their structure to assist them.

After the students have spent time working with specific resources, the librarians tell them about relevant search tips which could have made their research more efficient. Everything they are told about in the library session has a personal context. This approach has worked quite well, and instructing librarians have actually reported "ooohs and aaahs" from the students in these workshops!

This class was designed to allow five groups of students to present their research findings to the class, and for the librarian to respond to the presentations. We were able to fit the session into one 50-minute class.

Objectives of the Instruction:

- To teach search strategies specific to UW's on-line catalog,
- To teach search strategies for specific indexes, and
- To clarify differences between keyword and subject searches.

Components of the Library Instruction:

Part 1 Initial hands-on experience:

In our sessions, instructors prepared students for the initial hands-on portion of the assignment. Ideally, librarians would be involved in this process. Instructors choose one topic, divide students into six groups, and assign one or two specific reference sources to each group. The topic which is being used as the example is "Youth Violence."

Groups are divided and assigned sources as follows:

GROUPS	SOURCES
Group 1	*ERIC* *PsycINFO* (on-line)
Group 2	*Expanded Academic Index* *National Newspaper Index* (on-line)
Group 3	*Vital Speeches of the Day* *Congressional Record*
Group 4	*Statistical Abstracts* *Editorials on File* (print)
Group 5	*PAIS* (CD-ROM and print) *Sociofile* (CD-ROM)
Group 6	*CQ Researcher* *Congressional Digest* (print)

The students are told that the assignment is to inform the class about:

- where and how these resources can be accessed, and
- the type of information that might be useful.

Part 2   Classroom Presentations:

At the library session, each group takes approximately five minutes to speak about the resource they used and to demonstrate how they searched for the topic "Youth Violence" using the particular source. During these presentations, the librarian takes notes on search strategies that could be improved, misconceptions students have about sources, as well as excellent observations made by the students.

Part 3   Librarian Comments:

After all groups have reported, the librarian takes the center ring. She/He discusses each source again, encourages good search skills, mentions any misconceptions about sources, and offers ideas for making searches more efficient. Below are sample comments librarians would make, and following that are some points about the different sources that the librarian should cover.

Depending on time and assigned sources, librarians will vary the level of detail covered in each session. If there is time, the students appreciate demonstrations and overheads from print sources as visual aids. That can clarify source differences and searching tricks.

Sample comments by the librarian:

One student in Group 2 mentioned that all the newspapers indexed in the *National Newspaper Index* are also indexed in *Expanded Academic Index*. The librarian pointed out that more articles are indexed in the National Newspaper Index (demonstrate). For example, when I do a search in *Expanded Academic Index* using the keyword "bosnia" and the source as "new york times," I get a list of 16 articles. When I do the same search in *National Newspaper Index*, I get a list of 2906 articles.

Here's a time-saver for you. Did you notice when I changed databases, instead of hitting the QUIT AND RESTART button (demonstrate) as Group 2 demonstrated, I hit the DATABASE pull-down menu (demonstrate)? When I did this, my search was saved, so I didn't have to retype my search.

Group 2 also mentioned that when using *Expanded Academic Index*, they only found a few articles using the phrase "youth violence" in the KEYWORDS box (demonstrate and find 42 items). Let me show you a trick to finding more articles on youth violence in *Expanded Academic Index*. When I type in "youth and violence" I find even more articles (demonstrate and find 244 items). When you leave out the word "and," the computer matches the phrase "youth violence," but when you use "and" it looks for both words anywhere in the same abstract.

Someone in Group 6 mentioned that they found lots of articles with their search, but few were really relevant. Here's a trick you can use with most databases to weed out some of those false hits. See this area that says SUBJECT when you look at a record? Also notice how several of these articles have the phrase "violence in children?"

When I enter that phrase into a SUBJECT HEADING box for my search, rather than "youth and violence" in the KEYWORDS box, I cut down the number of records I get (demonstrate and find 63 items). But, also notice that they are more relevant to my specific topic.

Specialists at database headquarters assign subject headings after reading articles. The headings come from lists of official headings, so all articles on one topic will have the same heading. Using this heading applied by someone who's already read the article, is one way to be certain that articles are relevant to your research.

Remember to ask a librarian or library staff member for help or advice with your research. You don't have to wait until you're frustrated to ask for help but feel free to talk to a reference librarian before you begin your research.

General information the librarian should cover during class:

- Once you have articles that you want to find, you must check the on-line catalog to see

    (1) which UW library subscribes to the journal, magazine, or newspaper,

    (2) what years the library owns, and

    (3) the call number.

- Keyword (natural language) vs. subject headings (thesauri)
- Other searchable fields
- Boolean searching
- Synonyms and creative thinking
- Truncation
- E-mailing results to yourself rather than using printer paper
- Saving searches to use later
- Changing field codes (you can search using more criteria than you see immediately)

Information the librarian should cover for each source:

- Coverage

  types of materials
  years
  subjects

- Search techniques and tricks

- Truncation

- Classes or handouts available for each database

- Sample entries

- Differences between similar sources (example follows)

  Vital Speeches of the Day
  > Text of "important" speeches
  Congressional Record
  > Text of speeches given in Congress

Specific information the librarian should cover for each source:

Expanded Academic Index
- general interest topics
- magazines and scholarly journals
- 1989 to present
- search techniques similar to other UW on-line databases
- classes offered to teach this database

ERIC
- education-related information
- articles, documents, dissertations, classroom kits, unpublished materials
- 1969 to present
- search techniques similar to other UW on-line databases
- classes offered to teach this database

PsycINFO
- psychology and related fields
- articles in scholarly journals, technical reports, dissertations
- 1967 to present
- search techniques similar to other UW on-line databases
- classes offered to teach this database

National Newspaper Index
- 5 major U.S. newspapers: *New York Times, Wall Street Journal, Christian Science Monitor,Washington Post,* and *Los Angeles Times*
- not all articles indexed here, just some
- search techniques similar to other UW on-line databases

PAIS (Public Affairs Information Service)
- public affairs, public policy issues
- articles and official documents
- CD-ROM in Political Science Library, Print in Suzzallo Reference, Odegaard Undergraduate, and Social Work libraries

Newsbank
- 1970s to present
- two parts to Newsbank: CD-ROM index and microforms of articles
- use index to find articles on topic
- use microform to get articles

Ethnic Newswatch
- CD-ROM, full-text database
- articles from newspapers, magazines, and newsletters
- ethnic and religious communities in the US
- 1991 to present

New York Times Index
- print index to *New York Times*
- all articles indexed
- 1851 to present

Seattle Times Index
- CD-ROM, full-text database
- 1985 to present

Editorials on File
- Citations for editorials in newspapers

CQ Researcher(Congressional Quarterly Researcher)
- summaries of Congressional research reports (including a bibliography covering both viewpoints)

Congressional Digest
- major issues discussed in Congress
- includes speeches from congressmen and women

Statistical Abstract of the United States
- US government statistics in summary form

American Statistical Index (ASI)
- bibliography of US governmental statistical sources on specific topics
- index volume arranged by topic
- abstract volume provides summaries of articles

Statistical Reference Index (SRI)
- same format as *ASI* but for non-government statistical sources

Statistical Masterfile
- CD-ROM version of *ASI, SRI,* and *ISI* (international statistics sources)

Vital Speeches of the Day
- actual text of speeches
- indexed in *Expanded Academic Index*

Congressional Record
- actual text of speeches given in Congress

NOTES:

Examining Reference Sources

GAIL M. STAINES

Coordinator of Library Instruction
NIAGARA COUNTY COMMUNITY COLLEGE, SANBORN, NY

Circumstances for the Instruction Session:

Introducing first and second year undergraduate students to specialized reference sources is often one challenge library instruction librarians face. Reading an annotated bibliography of sources to students while holding a copy of each reference source in your hand (i.e. conducting a "book talk") can be tedious for the instructor and boring for the students. Below is a group exercise that can be integrated into almost any library instruction session. Although the example provided is specifically for literary criticism and biographical reference sources, reference sources in any discipline (i.e. business, psychology, sociology, technology, etc.) can be substituted.

Goal: Students enrolled in ENG 102: Writing II and Introduction to Literature are able to effectively search for biographical and literary criticism information.

Objectives of the Instruction:

Upon completion of this library instruction session:

- Students are familiar with literary criticism collections, both in Reference and the main collection.

- Students use the research strategy concept to locate literary criticism and biographical information about their authors and the authors' works.

- Students are able to search the on-line catalog for an author's works and for literary criticism.

- Students are familiar with indexes that cite biographical information and literary criticism, such as *INFOTRAC*, *The Humanities Index*, and *Essay and General Literature Index*.

- Students learn to analyze information through question analysis, asking questions such as:

  is the information relevant?
  is the information accurate?
  is the information appropriate?

Components of the Library Instruction:

Most students enrolled in ENG102 : Writing II and Introduction to Literature at Niagara County Community College are required to conduct a search for criticism on a specific work as well as locate biographical information about the author. Students can select works of poetry, short stories, novels, and essays from authors in any time period and from any geographic location. Students are usually given a choice of genres and a list of authors from which to select.

Library instruction is accomplished in one 50-minute or one 75-minute time block. This depends on the day of the week the class is offered (e.g.: Monday, Wednesday, Friday classes are 50-minutes, Tuesday and Thursday classes are 75 minutes). The first 10 to 15 minutes of this session provide background information to the students. During this time:

- the librarian and faculty member review the students' assignment;

- the librarian explains a research strategy for locating biographical and literary criticism information;

- a search for an author's works and literary criticism is completed on the on-line catalog; and

- students are asked if there are any questions about their assignment (this occurs throughout the session).

Hands-on Activity:

The allotment of time for the activity is about 15 minutes.

- Students are divided into groups

- Groups are created according to the tables where the students are seated; a maximum of 6 students are in each group

- The librarian asks the students to select one student in each group to take notes and another student to be a spokesperson

- Two copies of a reference book are distributed to each group. These can be biographical sources, such as: *Current Biography, Twentieth Century Authors, Contemporary Authors, Contemporary Authors, New Revision Series* and sources that contain criticism, such as *Contemporary Literary Criticism* or *Twentieth Century Literary Criticism*

Each group is given 7 to 10 minutes to answer seven questions about each source. A separate page has been included which lists these questions; that page can be used to make a transparency or to scan into presentation software such as PowerPoint.

- What is the title of the source?

- Who is the authority or author?

- What is the publication date?

- Is the source part of a series?

- What kinds of information are given?

- How can this source help you with your research?

- Does the source contain "help pages" (i.e.: table of contents, index, guide)?

The class then re-groups. The spokesperson shares answers to questions with the rest of the class. Students learn that reference sources are organized differently, such as by time period, genre, nationality, biography, criticism, etc. This exercise also gives students the opportunity to take time to examine, compare, and contrast reference sources interactively, thus alleviating some anxiety they may have about their project.

The librarian reviews the research strategy. An annotated list of reference sources (biographical and literary criticism) is provided to students. Students are given a few minutes to indicate sources they may want to use for their research. The librarian and faculty member ask if there are any more questions. Students are then taken to the reference area where the literary criticism sources are shelved to begin their research. The librarian and faculty member are available to help.

Evaluation:

Evaluation of this library instruction session is informal. Students receive a library instruction survey several weeks after the library instruction session. Students are asked for their reactions to the instruction and their perceptions concerning the librarian's preparedness for teaching. Feedback from these surveys along with observation indicates that this interactive instruction works well with students using sources more readily.

EXAMINING REFERENCE SOURCES

1. What is the title of the source?

2. Who is the authority or author?

3. What is the publication date?

4. Is the source part of a series?

5. What kinds of information are given?

6. How can this source help you with your research?

7. Does the source contain "help pages"
    table of contents?
    index?
    guide?

Activities Appropriate for 2 or 3 Students

This section contains:

Focusing Broad Topics
Marilyn P. Whitmore

Women's Studies
Charlene E. Hovatter

NOTES:

Focusing Broad Topics

MARILYN P. WHITMORE
Editor
LIBRARY INSTRUCTION PUBLICATIONS

Circumstances for the Instruction Session:

Library Instruction librarians are forever being asked to give library lectures with little advance notice. In many cases we have to suggest an alternative date because we are unprepared. However, if the classroom is available there might be circumstances when it is agreeable to go ahead with a session.

Few lower-level undergraduate students are skillful either focusing a topic or knowing where to begin searching for information sources. This chapter can be used as the structure for a lecture on how to focus a broad topic and then provide some hands-on experience.

Objectives of the Instruction:

- Reduce the anxiety level.
- Instill a methodology for getting a topic in focus.
- Raise the comfort level with a brief hands-on activity for teams.

Components of the Library Instruction:

Choose some method to form the class into pairs. Then ask them to become acquainted with each other for no more than five minutes. The librarian must control these five minutes by telling the students what to share about themselves.

Spend about half of the period discussing how to focus a topic and what it means to have a search strategy. An excellent book to use for background information is *Learning the Library,* by Beaubien, Hogan, and George (1982).

Hands-on Activities

Pass out **one copy** of the accompanying activity assignments to each pair. One copy only because that forces them to work together rather than individually and part of the learning process will be working and learning together.

The pairs are to select two of the questions asked on the activity sheet. The students should focus on these questions as they go through the steps. They are responsible for noting pertinent information that both of them can use to answer these questions.

The tasks of finding the reference sources can be achieved together, however, each member of the pair should use a different reference so that the assignment can move along quickly and they each do an equitable amount of the work.

It would be beneficial if the librarian arranges with the professor ahead of time to have the students finish the activity before the next class meeting. Then they could be prepared to discuss the experience and mention any difficulty.

Student hands-on activities cover the following 12 broad topics:

- Aging
- Air Pollution
- Fictional Detective
- Gun Control
- Juvenile Delinquency
- Press and Politics
- Sports and Society
- Television
- Terrorism
- United Nations
- Water Pollution
- Working Women

Research Topic: Juvenile Delinquency

This is a BROAD topic and you must develop a focus which is both interesting and workable to you. Use the questions below to help you decide on the focus for this assignment.

IS delinquent behavior more common in particular geographic areas or socio-economic groups?
HOW is it punished?
WHAT reforms are seen as necessary in the administration of juvenile justice?
WHAT factors contribute to the development of delinquency in modern society?
DO the same laws apply to adults and minors?

Ground Rules to follow during the search process:

- Keep a log so nothing has to be done twice.
- Print screens, or copy bibliographical details.
- Record all keywords you search.
- Record all reference works you search.

Step 1   Select and read from a general encyclopedia a background article about the topic. Always start with the index to locate the correct volume in which the articles(s) will be found. Often bibliographies are included at the end of the longer essays in general encyclopedias; evaluate these to see if any appear promising for the focus of your research.

Step 2   You may need to locate a specialized encyclopedia for more focused background than given in the general encyclopedia.

To identify these, do a keyword search in the on-line catalog. Combine the name of your discipline, sub-discipline or broad topic and the words (encyclopedias or dictionaries).

If you are not successful, ask for assistance from a member of library staff.

Step 3 Compile a list of keywords which you discovered now that you have read a couple of summary articles in encyclopedias. List as many as you can think of and consider revising them as you learn more about the topic.

_____   _____

_____   _____

_____   _____

_____   _____

Step 4 Search for some ready-made bibliographies in the *Bibliographic Index* and also in the on-line catalog. Search by keyword. In the on-line catalog, add the word bibliography to a keyword in order to see if there are any full-length books on the topic.

Step 5 Now, you need to think about fields or disciplines. Ask yourself which disciplines would have published articles and reports on your research topic. Consult with library staff for assistance.

DISCIPLINE   INDEX or ABSTRACT

_____   _____

_____   _____

Step 6 Search a general periodical index to locate articles which have a popular or mass-audience point of view. Use the keywords from your list.

Periodical Abstracts and *Expanded Academic Index* are two general periodical indexes in electronic format; each provides access to more than a thousand "high demand" magazines and journals. Coverage begins about the mid–1980s and you can expect to find some articles on almost any topic you choose. If your library doesn't have access to an electronic title, use *Readers' Guide to Periodical Literature*. This title indexes articles in about 200 magazines which are popular in nature. Also, use the *Readers' Guide* for earlier coverage when you need information published before the mid–1980s.

Research Topic: Sports and Society

This is a BROAD topic and you must develop a focus which is both interesting and workable to you. Use the questions below to help you decide on the focus for this assignment.

WHAT are some of the psychological and sociological aspects of being a participant or spectator of sports?

HOW AND WHY have some sports ceased to be "fun" and become big business?

IS violence in sports becoming excessive?

WHAT are the advantages and disadvantages of amateur versus professional status in various sports?

HOW important are sports and its heroes to the public?

DO world political conflicts endanger international sports competitions such as the Olympics and similar events?

Ground Rules to follow during the search process:

- Keep a log so nothing has to be done twice.
- Print screens, or copy bibliographical details.
- Record all keywords you search.
- Record all reference works you search.

Step 1   Select and read from a general encyclopedia a background article about the topic Always start with the index to locate the correct volume in which the articles(s) will be found. Often bibliographies are included at the end of the longer essays in general encyclopedias; evaluate these to see if any appear promising for the focus of your research.

Step 2   You may need to locate a specialized encyclopedia for more focused background than given in the general encyclopedia.

To identify these, do a keyword search in the on-line catalog. Combine the name of your discipline, sub-discipline or broad topic and the words (encyclopedias or dictionaries).

Step 3   Compile a list of keywords which you discovered now that you have read a
          couple of summary articles in encyclopedias. List as many as you can think of
          and consider revising them as you learn more about the topic.

_____   _____

_____   _____

_____   _____

Step 4   Search for some ready-made bibliographies in the *Bibliographic Index* and also
          in the on-line catalog. Search by keyword.

          In the on-line catalog, add the word bibliography to a keyword in order to see if
          there are any full-length books on the topic.

Step 5   Now you need to think about fields or disciplines. Ask yourself which
          disciplines would have published articles and reports on your research topic.
          Consult with library staff about those you have chosen and ask the names of the
          indexes or databases to search.

          DISCIPLINE   INDEX or ABSTRACT

_____   _____

_____   _____

Step 6   Search a general periodical index to locate articles which have a popular or
          mass-audience point of view. Use the keywords from your list.

          Periodical Abstracts and *Expanded Academic Index* are two general periodical
          indexes in electronic format; each provides access to more than a thousand "high
          demand" magazines and journals. Coverage begins about the mid–1980s and you
          can expect to find some articles on almost any topic you choose. If your library
          doesn't have access to an electronic title, use *Readers' Guide to Periodical
          Literature*. This title indexes articles in about 200 magazines which are popular in
          nature. Also, use the *Readers' Guide* for earlier coverage when you need
          information published before the mid–1980s.

Research Topic: Air Pollution

This is a BROAD topic and you must develop a focus which is both interesting and workable to you. Use the questions below to help you decide on the focus for this assignment.

WHAT are the major causes of air pollution?
WHAT are solutions?
WHAT economic problems are involved?
WHAT are the health hazards posed by air pollution?
WHAT has been the government's response? Industry's response?
WHAT relation does air pollution have to the "greenhouse effect"?

Ground Rules to follow during the search process:

- Keep a log so nothing has to be done twice.
- Print screens, or copy bibliographical details.
- Record all keywords you search.
- Record all reference works you search.

Step 1   Select and read from a general encyclopedia a background article about the topic. Always start with the index to locate the correct volume in which the articles(s) will be found. Often bibliographies are included at the end of the longer essays in general encyclopedias; evaluate these to see if any appear promising for the focus of your research.

Step 2   You may need to locate a specialized encyclopedia for more focused background than given in the general encyclopedia.

To identify these, do a keyword search in the on-line catalog. Combine the name of your discipline, sub-discipline or broad topic and the words (encyclopedias or dictionaries).

If you are not successful, ask for assistance from a member of library staff.

Step 3 Compile a list of keywords which you discovered now that you have read a couple of summary articles in encyclopedias. List as many as you can think of and consider revising them as you learn more about the topic.

_____   _____

_____   _____

_____   _____

_____

Step 4 Search for some ready-made bibliographies in the *Bibliographic Index* and also in the on-line catalog. Search by keyword. In the on-line catalog, add the word bibliography to a keyword in order to see if there are any full-length books.

Step 5 Now you need to think about fields or disciplines. Ask yourself which disciplines would have published articles and reports on your research topic. Consult with library staff about those you have chosen and ask the names of the indexes or databases to search.

DISCIPLINE   INDEX or ABSTRACT

_____   _____

_____   _____

Step 6 Search a general periodical index to locate articles which have a popular or mass-audience point of view. Use the keywords from your list.

Periodical Abstracts and *Expanded Academic Index* are two general periodical indexes in electronic format; each provides access to more than a thousand "high demand" magazines and journals. Coverage begins about the mid–1980s and you can expect to find some articles on almost any topic you choose. If your library doesn't have access to an electronic title, use *Readers' Guide to Periodical Literature*. This title indexes articles in about 200 magazines which are popular in nature. Also, use the *Readers' Guide* for earlier coverage when you need information published before the mid–1980s.

Research Topic: Water Pollution

This is a BROAD topic and you must develop a focus which is both interesting and workable to you. Use the questions below to help you decide on the focus for this assignment.

WHEN did water pollution become an issue?

WHAT are some of the causes and results of water pollution?

WHAT has been the government's response to the problem? Industry's response?

HOW does the average household contribute to water pollution?

HOW safe are most municipal water supplies?

Ground Rules to follow during the search process:

- Keep a log so nothing has to be done twice.
- Print screens, or copy bibliographical details.
- Record all keywords you search.
- Record all reference works you search.

Step 1 Select and read from a general encyclopedia a background article about the topic. Always start with the index to locate the correct volume in which the articles(s) will be found. Often bibliographies are included at the end of the longer essays in general encyclopedias; evaluate these to see if any appear promising for the focus of your research.

Step 2 You may need to locate a specialized encyclopedia for more focused background than given in the general encyclopedia.

To identify these, do a keyword search in the on-line catalog. Combine the name of your discipline, sub-discipline or broad topic and the words (encyclopedias or dictionaries).

If you are not successful, ask for assistance from a member of library staff.

Step 3   Compile a list of keywords which you discovered now that you have read a couple of summary articles in encyclopedias. List as many as you can think of and consider revising them as you learn more about the topic.

_____   _____

_____   _____

_____   _____

Step 4   Search for some ready-made bibliographies in the *Bibliographic Index* and also in the on-line catalog. Search by keyword. In the on-line catalog, add the word bibliography to a keyword in order to see if there are any full-length books on the topic.

Step 5   Now you need to think about fields or disciplines. Ask yourself which disciplines would have published articles and reports on your research topic. Consult with library staff about those you have chosen and ask the names of the indexes or databases to search.

DISCIPLINE   INDEX or ABSTRACT

_____   _____

_____   _____

Step 6   Search a general periodical index to locate articles which have a popular or mass-audience point of view. Use the keywords from your list.

Periodical Abstracts and *Expanded Academic Index* are two general periodical indexes in electronic format; each provides access to more than a thousand "high demand" magazines and journals. Coverage begins about the mid–1980s and you can expect to find some articles on almost any topic you choose. If your library doesn't have access to an electronic title, use *Readers' Guide to Periodical Literature*. This title indexes articles in about 200 magazines which are popular in nature. Also, use the *Readers' Guide* for earlier coverage when you need information published before the mid–1980s.

STUDENT(S)..

Research Topic: Gun Control

This is a BROAD topic and you must develop a focus which is both interesting andworkable to you. Use the questions below to help you decide on the focus for this assignment.

WHAT are the arguments for and against gun control?

DOES the availability of guns lead to their use in crime?

HOW is the phrase "the right to bear arms" interpreted by the National Rifle Association or by gun control advocates?

WHY is gun control such a controversial issue in the US when it is practiced successfully in many other countries?

Ground Rules to follow during the search process:

- Keep a log so nothing has to be done twice.
- Print screens, or copy bibliographical details.
- Record all keywords you search.
- Record all reference works you search.

Step 1   Select and read from a general encyclopedia a background article about the topic. Always start with the index to locate the correct volume in which the articles(s will be found). Often bibliographies are included at the end of the longer essays in general encyclopedias; evaluate these to see if any appear promising for the focus of your research.

Step 2   You may need to locate a specialized encyclopedia for more focused background than given in the general encyclopedia.

To identify these, do a keyword search in the on-line catalog. Combine the name of your discipline, sub-discipline or broad topic and the words (encyclopedias or dictionaries).

If you are not successful, ask for assistance from a member of library staff.

Step 3   Compile a list of keywords which you discovered now that you have read a
          couple of summary articles in encyclopedias. List as many as you can think of
          and consider revising them as you learn more about the topic.

          _____   _____

          _____   _____

          _____   _____

Step 4   Search for some ready-made bibliographies in the *Bibliographic Index* and also
          in the on-line catalog. Search by keyword. In the on-line catalog, add the word
          bibliography to a keyword in order to see if there are any full-length books on
          the topic.

Step 5   Now you need to think about fields or disciplines. Ask yourself which
          disciplines would have published articles and reports on your research topic.
          Consult with library staff about those you have chosen and ask the names of the
          indexes or databases to search.

          DISCIPLINE   INDEX or ABSTRACT

          _____   _____

          _____   _____

Step 6   Search a general periodical index to locate articles which have a popular or
          mass-audience point of view. Use the keywords from your list.

          Periodical Abstracts and *Expanded Academic Index* are two general periodical
          indexes in electronic format; each provides access to more than a thousand "high
          demand" magazines and journals. Coverage begins about the mid–1980s and you
          can expect to find some articles on almost any topic you choose.

          If your library doesn't have access to an electronic title, use *Readers' Guide to
          Periodical Literature*. This title indexes articles in about 200 magazines which are
          popular in nature. Also, use the *Readers' Guide* for earlier coverage when you
          need information published before the mid–1980s.

Research Topic: Terrorism

This is a BROAD topic and you must develop a focus which is both interesting and workable to you. Use the questions below to help you decide on the focus for this assignment.

HAS terrorism become more prevalent in the world today? Why?
How is terrorism used as a means to political ends?
WHAT is the relationship between terrorism and revolution?
WHAT can nations do to protect citizens from terrorist attacks?
WHAT are the moral and ethical considerations of terrorist activity?
How has assassination been used as a terrorist tool?

Ground Rules to follow during the search process:

- Keep a log so nothing has to be done twice.
- Print screens, or copy bibliographical details.
- Record all keywords you search.
- Record all reference works you search.

Step 1   Select and read from a general encyclopedia a background article about the topic. Always start with the index to locate the correct volume in which the articles(s) will be found. Often bibliographies are included at the end of the longer essays in general encyclopedias; evaluate these to see if any appear promising for the focus of your research.

Step 2   You may need to locate a specialized encyclopedia for more focused background than given in the general encyclopedia.

To identify these, do a keyword search in the on-line catalog. Combine the name of your discipline, sub-discipline or broad topic and the words (encyclopedias or dictionaries).

If you are not successful, ask for assistance from a member of library staff.

Step 3   Compile a list of keywords which you discovered now that you have read a couple of summary articles in encyclopedias. List as many as you can think of and consider revising them as you learn more about the topic.

_____   _____

_____   _____

_____   _____

_____   _____

Step 4   Search for some ready-made bibliographies in the *Bibliographic Index* and also in the on-line catalog. Search by keyword. In the on-line catalog, add the word bibliography to a keyword in order to see if there are any full-length books on the topic.

Step 5   Now you need to think about fields or disciplines. Ask yourself which disciplines would have published articles and reports on your research topic. Consult with library staff about those you have chosen and ask the names of the indexes or databases to search.

DISCIPLINE   INDEX or ABSTRACT

_____   _____

_____   _____

Step 6   Search a general periodical index to locate articles which have a popular or mass-audience point of view. Use the keywords from your list.

Periodical Abstracts and *Expanded Academic Index* are two general periodical indexes in electronic format; each provides access to more than a thousand "high demand" magazines and journals. Coverage begins about the mid–1980s and you can expect to find some articles on almost any topic you choose.

If your library doesn't have access to an electronic title, use *Readers' Guide to Periodical Literature*. This title indexes articles in about 200 magazines which are popular in nature. Also, use the *Readers' Guide* for earlier coverage when you need information published before the mid–1980s.

Research Topic: The United Nations

This is a BROAD topic and you must develop a focus which is both interesting and workable to you. Use the questions below to help you decide on the focus for this assignment.

HOW well has the United Nations fulfilled its original purposes?
IS the UN out of date?
HOW effective is the UN as a peacekeeping organization?
WHY is the UN unpopular with some groups in the United States?
IF the UN is to survive, what needs to be done to make it a strong power in world affairs?

Ground Rules to follow during the search process:

- Keep a log so nothing has to be done twice.
- Print screens, or copy bibliographical details.
- Record all keywords you search.
- Record all reference works you search.

Step 1   Select and read from a general encyclopedia a background article about the topic. Always start with the index to locate the correct volume in which the articles(s) will be found. Often bibliographies are included at the end of the longer essays in general encyclopedias; evaluate these to see if any appear promising for the focus of your research.

Step 2   You may need to locate a specialized encyclopedia for more focused background than given in the general encyclopedia.

To identify these, do a keyword search in the on-line catalog. Combine the name of your discipline, sub-discipline or broad topic and the words (encyclopedias or dictionaries).

If you are not successful, ask for assistance from a member of library staff.

Step 3   Compile a list of keywords which you discovered now that you have read a couple of summary articles in encyclopedias. List as many as you can think of and consider revising them as you learn more about the topic.

_____   _____

_____   _____

_____   _____

Step 4   Search for some ready-made bibliographies in the *Bibliographic Index* and also in the on-line catalog. Search by keyword. In the on-line catalog, add the word bibliography to a keyword in order to see if there are any full-length books on the topic.

Step 5   Now you need to think about fields or disciplines. Ask yourself which disciplines would have published articles and reports on your research topic. Consult with library staff about those you have chosen and ask the names of the indexes or databases to search.

DISCIPLINE   INDEX or ABSTRACT

_____   _____

_____   _____

Step 6   Search a general periodical index to locate articles which have a popular or mass-audience point of view. Use the keywords from your list.

Periodical Abstracts and *Expanded Academic Index* are two general periodical indexes in electronic format; each provides access to more than a thousand "high demand" magazines and journals. Coverage begins about the mid–1980s and you can expect to find some articles on almost any topic you choose.

If your library doesn't have access to an electronic title, use *Readers' Guide to Periodical Literature*. This title indexes articles in about 200 magazines which are popular in nature. Also, use the *Readers' Guide* for earlier coverage when you need information published before the mid–1980s.

STUDENT(S)...

Research Topic: The Press and Politics

This is a BROAD topic and you must develop a focus which is both interesting and workable to you. Use the questions below to help you decide on the focus for this assignment.

WHAT effect does television and radio coverage have on elections?

HAVE campaign strategies changed as a result?

DOES television, radio, and newspaper coverage make politicians more open to ridicule and scandal?

WHAT effect does television, radio, and newspaper coverage have on political events?

IS legislation to control the political use of the press desirable?

CAN the press "make" or "break" a political figure?

DOES media coverage have an effect on the results of presidential elections?

Ground Rules to follow during the search process:

- Keep a log so nothing has to be done twice.
- Print screens, or copy bibliographical details.
- Record all keywords you search.
- Record all reference works you search.

Step 1   Select and read from a general encyclopedia a background article about the topic. Always start with the index to locate the correct volume in which the articles(s) will be found. Often bibliographies are included at the end of the longer essays in general encyclopedias; evaluate these to see if any appear promising for the focus of your research.

Step 2   You may need to locate a specialized encyclopedia for more focused background than given in the general encyclopedia.

To identify these, do a keyword search in the on-line catalog. Combine the name of your discipline, sub-discipline or broad topic and the words (encyclopedias or dictionaries).

If you are not successful, ask for assistance from a member of library staff.

Step 3   Compile a list of keywords which you discovered now that you have read a couple of summary articles in encyclopedias. List as many as you can think of and consider revising them as you learn more about the topic.

_____   _____

_____   _____

_____   _____

Step 4   Search for some ready-made bibliographies in the *Bibliographic Index* and also in the on-line catalog. Search by keyword. in the on-line catalog, add the word bibliography to a keyword in order to see if there are any full-length books on the topic.

Step 5   Now you need to think about fields or disciplines. Ask yourself which disciplines would have published articles and reports on your research topic. Consult with library staff about those you have chosen and ask the names of the indexes or databases to search.

DISCIPLINE   INDEX or ABSTRACT

_____   _____

_____   _____

Step 6   Search a general periodical index to locate articles which have a popular or mass-audience point of view. Use the keywords from your list.

Periodical Abstracts and *Expanded Academic Index* are two general periodical indexes in electronic format; each provides access to more than a thousand "high demand" magazines and journals. Coverage begins about the mid–1980s and you can expect to find some articles on almost any topic you choose.

If your library doesn't have access to an electronic title, use *Readers' Guide to Periodical Literature*. This title indexes articles in about 200 magazines which are popular in nature. Also, use the *Readers' Guide* for earlier coverage when you need information published before the mid–1980s.

STUDENT(S)..

Research Topic: Aging

This is a BROAD topic and you must develop a focus which is both interesting and workable to you. Use the questions below to help you decide on the focus for this assignment.

WHAT is it like to be old in the US?
HOW is the age distribution of the population changing?
WHAT problems in income, housing, or medical care do older people face?
HOW does treatment of older people differ in other countries?
WHAT factors in our culture contribute to our attitude toward old age?
WHAT is "gray power"?

Ground Rules to follow during the search process:

- Keep a log so nothing has to be done twice.
- Print screens, or copy bibliographical details.
- Record all keywords you search.
- Record all reference works you search.

Step 1   Select and read from a general encyclopedia a background article about the topic. Always start with the index to locate the correct volume in which the articles(s) will be found. Often bibliographies are included at the end of the longer essays in general encyclopedias; evaluate these to see if any appear promising for the focus of your research.

Step 2   You may need to locate a specialized encyclopedia for more focused background than given in the general encyclopedia.

To identify these, do a keyword search in the on-line catalog. Combine the name of your discipline, sub-discipline or broad topic and the words (encyclopedias or dictionaries).

If you are not successful, ask for assistance from a member of library staff.

Step 3   Compile a list of keywords which you discovered now that you have read a
couple of summary articles in encyclopedias. List as many as you can think of
and consider revising them as you learn more about the topic.

_____   _____

_____   _____

_____   _____

Step 4   Search for some ready-made bibliographies in the *Bibliographic Index* and also
in the on-line catalog. Search by keyword. In the on-line catalog, add the word
bibliography to a keyword in order to see if there are any full-length books on
the topic.

Step 5   Now you need to think about fields or disciplines. Ask yourself which
disciplines would have published articles and reports on your research topic.
Consult with library staff about those you have chosen and ask the names of the
indexes or databases to search.

DISCIPLINE   INDEX or ABSTRACT

_____   _____

_____   _____

Step 6   Search a general periodical index to locate articles which have a popular or
mass-audience point of view. Use the keywords from your list.

Periodical Abstracts and *Expanded Academic Index* are two general periodical
indexes in electronic format; each provides access to more than a thousand "high
demand" magazines and journals. Coverage begins about the mid–1980s and you
can expect to find some articles on almost any topic you choose.

If your library doesn't have access to an electronic title, use *Readers' Guide to
Periodical Literature*. This title indexes articles in about 200 magazines which are
popular in nature. Also, use the *Readers' Guide* for earlier coverage when you
need information published before the mid–1980s.

Research Topic: Working Women

This is a BROAD topic and you must develop a focus which is both interesting and workable to you. Use the questions below to help you decide on the focus for this assignment.

WHAT are the special needs or problems of blue collar women workers? White collar?

CAN a woman be employed and raise children successfully at the same time?

HAVE men assumed equal responsibility for the care of their children?

WHAT can be done to make maintaining a career easier for working mothers? Is daycare the answer?

HAVE affirmative action programs helped women facing discrimination in employment to get jobs? To get promoted?

Ground Rules to follow during the search process:

- Keep a log so nothing has to be done twice.
- Print screens, or copy bibliographical details.
- Record all keywords you search.
- Record all reference works you search.

Step 1   Select and read from a general encyclopedia a background article about the topic. Always start with the index to locate the correct volume in which the articles(s) will be found. Often bibliographies are included at the end of the longer essays in general encyclopedias; evaluate these to see if any appear promising for the focus of your research.

Step 2   You may need to locate a specialized encyclopedia for more focused background than given in the general encyclopedia.

To identify these, do a keyword search in the on-line catalog. Combine the name of your discipline, sub-discipline or broad topic and the words (encyclopedias or dictionaries).

If you are not successful, ask for assistance from a member of library staff.

Step 3   Compile a list of keywords which you discovered now that you have read a
          couple of summary articles in encyclopedias. List as many as you can think of
          and consider revising them as you learn more about the topic.

_____   _____

_____   _____

_____   _____

Step 4   Search for some ready-made bibliographies in the *Bibliographic Index* and also
          in the on-line catalog. Search by keyword. In the on-line catalog, add the word
          bibliography to a keyword in order to see if there are any full-length books on
          the topic.

Step 5   Now you need to think about fields or disciplines. Ask yourself which
          disciplines would have published articles and reports on your research topic.
          Consult with library staff about those you have chosen and ask the names of the
          indexes or databases to search.

DISCIPLINE   INDEX or ABSTRACT

_____   _____

_____   _____

Step 6   Search a general periodical index to locate articles which have a popular or
          mass-audience point of view. Use the keywords from your list.

          Periodical Abstracts and *Expanded Academic Index* are two general periodical
          indexes in electronic format; each provides access to more than a thousand "high
          demand" magazines and journals. Coverage begins about the mid–1980s and you
          can expect to find some articles on almost any topic you choose.

          If your library doesn't have access to an electronic title, use *Readers' Guide to
          Periodical Literature*. This title indexes articles in about 200 magazines which are
          popular in nature. Also, use the *Readers' Guide* for earlier coverage when you
          need information published before the mid–1980s.

Research Topic: The Fictional Detective

This is a BROAD topic and you must develop a focus which is both interesting and workable to you. Use the questions below to help you decide on the focus for this assignment.

WHEN did the detective story become popular?

WHY has it remained popular?

WHO were the early detective fiction writers and what characters did they create?

WHAT characteristics do these characters have in common with current detectives?

HOW have famous detective characters reflected the attitudes of their times?

HOW has the detective and mystery fiction changed since 1940?

Ground Rules to follow during the search process:

- Keep a log so nothing has to be done twice.
- Print screens, or copy bibliographical details.
- Record all keywords you search.
- Record all reference works you search.

Step 1   Select and read from a general encyclopedia a background article about the topic. Always start with the index to locate the correct volume in which the articles(s) will be found. Often bibliographies are included at the end of the longer essays in general encyclopedias; evaluate these to see if any appear promising for the focus of your research.

Step 2   You may need to locate a specialized encyclopedia for more focused background than given in the general encyclopedia.

To identify these, do a keyword search in the on-line catalog. Combine the name of your discipline, sub-discipline or broad topic and the words (encyclopedias or dictionaries).

If you are not successful, ask for assistance from a member of library staff.

Step 3   Compile a list of keywords which you discovered now that you have read a couple of summary articles in encyclopedias. List as many as you can think of and consider revising them as you learn more about the topic.

_____   _____

_____   _____

_____   _____

Step 4   Search for some ready-made bibliographies in the *Bibliographic Index* and also in the on-line catalog. Search by keyword. In the on-line catalog, add the word bibliography to a keyword in order to see if there are any full-length books on the topic.

Step 5   Now you need to think about fields or disciplines. Ask yourself which disciplines would have published articles and reports on your research topic. Consult with library staff about those you have chosen and ask the names of the indexes or databases to search.

DISCIPLINE   INDEX or ABSTRACT

_____   _____

_____   _____

Step 6   Search a general periodical index to locate articles which have a popular or mass-audience point of view. Use the keywords from your list.

Periodical Abstracts and *Expanded Academic Index* are two general periodical indexes in electronic format; each provides access to more than a thousand "high demand" magazines and journals. Coverage begins about the mid–1980s and you can expect to find some articles on almost any topic you choose.

If your library doesn't have access to an electronic title, use *Readers' Guide to Periodical Literature*. This title indexes articles in about 200 magazines which are popular in nature. Also, use the *Readers' Guide* for earlier coverage when you need information published before the mid–1980s.

Research Topic: Television

This is a BROAD topic and you must develop a focus which is both interesting and workable to you. Use the questions below to help you decide on the focus for this assignment.

WHY does television violence affect the public?

HOW do TV watchers differ from non-watchers?

WHAT can children learn from television?

WHO determines what appears on television: advertisers, producers, network officials, the public?

HOW has television programming changed over the years ?

WHAT impact does cable TV have on television viewers? On the television industry?

Ground Rules to follow during the search process:

- Keep a log so nothing has to be done twice.
- Print screens, or copy bibliographical details.
- Record all keywords you search.
- Record all reference works you search.

Step 1   Select and read from a general encyclopedia a background article about the topic. Always start with the index to locate the correct volume in which the articles(s) will be found. Often bibliographies are included at the end of the longer essays in general encyclopedias; evaluate these to see if any appear promising for the focus of your research.

Step 2   You may need to locate a specialized encyclopedia for more focused background than given in the general encyclopedia.

To identify these, do a keyword search in the on-line catalog. Combine the name of your discipline, sub-discipline or broad topic and the words (encyclopedias or dictionaries).

If you are not successful, ask for assistance from a member of library staff.

Step 3   Compile a list of keywords which you discovered now that you have read a
          couple of summary articles in encyclopedias. List as many as you can think of
          and consider revising them as you learn more about the topic.

_____   _____

_____   _____

_____   _____

Step 4   Search for some ready-made bibliographies in the *Bibliographic Index* and also
          in the on-line catalog. Search by keyword. In the on-line catalog, add the word
          bibliography to a keyword in order to see if there are any full-length books on
          the topic.

Step 5   Now you need to think about fields or disciplines. Ask yourself which
          disciplines would have published articles and reports on your research topic.
          Consult with library staff about those you have chosen and ask the names of the
          indexes or databases to search.

DISCIPLINE   INDEX or ABSTRACT

_____   _____

_____   _____

Step 6   Search a general periodical index to locate articles which have a popular or
          mass-audience point of view. Use the keywords from your list.

          Periodical Abstracts and *Expanded Academic Index* are two general periodical
          indexes in electronic format; each provides access to more than a thousand "high
          demand" magazines and journals. Coverage begins about the mid–1980s and you
          can expect to find some articles on almost any topic you choose.

          If your library doesn't have access to an electronic title, use *Readers' Guide to
          Periodical Literature*. This title indexes articles in about 200 magazines which are
          popular in nature. Also, use the *Readers' Guide* for earlier coverage when you
          need information published before the mid–1980s.

Women's Studies

CHARLENE E. HOVATTER
Library Instruction Librarian
UNIVERSITY OF PITTSBURGH

Circumstances for the Instruction Session:

Research in Women's Studies can be a difficult and time consuming task compared to research conducted in more well-established fields. The reasons for this are numerous. The field is relatively new in academia and has not yet achieved widespread acceptance. Therefore, many indexing and abstracting tools are unlikely to include any but the most well-known journals in women's studies. Mainstream magazine indexes will not pick up many of the smaller, non-commercial magazines, newsletters, and newspapers that make up the bulk of primary source materials related to events within the women's movement.

Furthermore, women's studies is an interdisciplinary field, and thus, sources for a particular topic may be drawn from the literature of several fields. This requires that the student consult many more reference sources than a student whose topic is restricted to the field of psychology or sociology. Finally, the problem of women's names and identity often hampers the research process. When searching for information about women, students must often search under both maiden and married names. If the person has married and changed names more than once, the problem multiplies. Also, the history of paternalism in many cultures has resulted in difficulty defining the national identity of women as separate from that of their families. For instance, works regarding a poet who lived all her life in England might be found in the MLA Bibliography under Irish literature if her father were from Ireland. This is perhaps *the* most frustrating aspect of women's studies research. The illusory nature of women's names and identities often very effectively hides them from history, and only the most diligent researcher can uncover the remnants of their past.

All of this can be very frustrating for beginning researchers trying to find relevant information in the field of women's studies. However, those studying women's studies often have a personal interest in the topic, enhancing the sense of discovery they experience in finding new materials and strengthening their resolve to dig deeper to find the information they need. And ironically, the very difficulty researchers find in accessing these materials reinforces the need for further research in this area, both to bring the subject into the mainstream of academia and to ensure that scholarly work dealing with women will never again become this inaccessible to researchers.

Objectives of the Instruction:

- Students will critically evaluate LC Subject Headings, key terms, and reference resources according to usefulness and relevancy to their search topics

- Students will use keywords and LC Subject Headings to find materials in the on-line catalog

- Students will use keyword terms and identify descriptors for finding citations to articles in indexing tools

- Students will identify and use reference materials to find background information on a topic

- Students will successfully navigate complex research tools

- Students will understand the differences between subject and keyword searching

- Students will use call numbers to locate books on the shelf

Components of the Library Instruction:

The exercises will be preceded by a library instruction session which introduces some essential library research tools, such as the on-line or card catalog, major indexes and abstracts, and basic references sources in women's studies. This session should also briefly outline some of the problems associated with conducting research in this field.

Hands-on Activities:

The following exercises are designed to illustrate some examples of common research problems in women's studies. These exercises will be most beneficial if a team approach is used, with groups of 2–3 students working together. Also, the students should have an opportunity to share their findings in completing the exercises with the rest of the class. This "jigsaw" type technique will greatly enhance the learning process and demonstrate a large variety of situations for the students involved.

For students who want a more in-depth introduction to women's studies research, I highly recommend Susan Searing's *Introduction to Library Research in Women's Studies*, published in 1985 by Westview Press, Boulder, CO. I am indebted to Susan Searing, as I borrowed much of the information above from the Introduction to this work.

STUDENT(S)..

Library Research Exercise

Historical approaches to the prevention of teenage pregnancy

Find books and other relevant materials dealing with this research topic

Step 1   When you begin to search for books and other materials on a topic, it is wise to think about possible keywords which can be used to access your subject. Write down some keywords for this topic:

    _____   _____

    _____   _____

    _____   _____

    _____   _____

Although most library catalogs allow searching by keyword, it is also sometimes useful to know the *Library of Congress Subject Headings* for your topic. These headings are assigned to subjects by the Library of Congress and are used in most US libraries. They are a fail-safe access point for searching, as all items on a topic will have been assigned the appropriate subject heading(s). Knowing these headings takes a lot of the guess work out of keyword searching.

Step 2   Find a recent copy of the *Library of Congress Subject Headings* (*LCSH*). Ask for help at the Reference Desk if you can't find them. Subject Headings are listed alphabetically in this reference source. Look up the term "teenage pregnancy" in the appropriate volume. Under the bold letter heading, you will notice some other words in lighter print with bold codes to their left. These are "see also" references and may give you ideas on different terms to use. The meaning of the codes are as follows:

UF   "use for" or "use 'teenage pregnancy' instead of this term"
NT   a "narrower term" for this topic than "teenage pregnancy"
BT   a "broader term" for this topic than "teenage pregnancy"
RT   a "related term" to "teenage pregnancy"

Write down any broader, related, or narrower terms you find:

_____   _____

_____   _____

Did you find any terms that might fit your topic, but that surprised you or you didn't have in your keyword list? What are they, if any?

_____   _____

Did you find any terms that are either too broad or narrow or won't be useful for your search? If so, what are they?

_____   _____

Step 3   Now, go to the on-line catalog and try a keyword search using the terms "teenage pregnancy" and "prevention." How many items did you find?_____

Print a record or write down the title and call number for a book that looks relevant to this topic.

_____

_____

Try another keyword search with one of the useful terms you found in *LCSH* and "prevention." How many items did you find this time?_____ If you found any, print a record or copy the information for one of the books.

_____

_____

Try a subject search on "teenage pregnancy" and then on one of the terms you found using *LCSH*. Do you notice any differences in the number and/or the nature of the items retrieved by these two searches?_____ If so, list them briefly here:

_____

_____

_____

Do you think that *LCSH* is a useful tool for scholars doing library research in women's studies and in other fields?_____ Briefly explain why or why not you find it useful.

_____

_____

_____

Step 4   What if you also wanted to find periodical articles on this topic? You can't find references to articles in the on-line catalog, so you will have to go to indexes and abstracts. Many topics in women's studies are interdisciplinary, meaning that you will find references to one topic in the literature of many fields. Of course, women's studies has its own tools for indexing journals, but often these won't pick up relevant articles from journals in other disciplines.

Listed below are indexes and abstracts which are commonly held by libraries in either paper or electronic form. Rank this list from 1–6, with 1 being the most relevant to this topic, and 6 being the least relevant.

_____*Psychological Abstracts*   _____*Sociological Abstracts*
_____*P.A.I.S.* (public affairs)   _____*Applied Science & Tech. Index*
_____*ERIC* (education index)   _____*Women's Studies Abstracts*

Step 5   Find one of these indexes in paper or electronic form, and conduct a search using one of the *LCSH* terms. While most on-line catalogs use *LCSH*, most indexes and abstracts have their own listings of subject headings that are different from those in *LCSH*. Did you find any new terms to use in your searching?_____ If so, write them down here:

_____   _____

Write down or print out one of the citations to an article which you found in the index or abstract. (Hint: some of these sources index other types of materials, as well as journal articles.)

_____

_____

Please hand in this exercise sheet, along with your notes or prints, to your instructor!

Library Research Exercise

Conduct a comparative examination of two indexes regarding coverage of women's studies information.

The Arts and Humanities Citation Index (AHCI) is a complex, yet very useful tool. The unique function of this tool is that it allows you to see who has cited a particular author or work. Generally, scholars regard it as very thorough in it's indexing of the major journals in all fields of the humanities. It is useful if you want to see how different scholars have interpreted a work and referred to it in their writings. It can also be used to judge how influential a scholar is in his or her field, by noting the frequency with which they have been cited by others. For this reason, AHCI is often used by tenure and promotional committees to judge a scholar's work.

While AHCI covers some feminist and women's studies journals, it unfortunately also neglects some important women's studies journals, spelling possible disaster for the scholars who publish in these journals.

Step 1   Find the *AHCI* in its paper form (ask at the reference desk if you need help). Each year has several different volumes. Pick a recent volume which says "Citation Index" at the top of the spine. Near the front of this volume, there is a list of fully and selectively covered source publications listed by full title. Look to see if *Hypatia: A Journal of Feminist Philosophy* is included in this list.

Is it listed? _____

Can you find the feminist journal *Signs* in the list? _____

Now, look in the introduction at the front of this volume and see if there is any information about how and why items are selected for indexing and what kind of items are included in the listing you just consulted. List some reasons why *Signs* and/or *Hypatia* may or may not have been included in the list.

_____

_____

If *Hypatia* is the primary journal for the publication of feminist philosophy and if it is not indexed by *AHCI*, how might this affect someone doing research on the frequency with which a particular feminist scholar in the field of philosophy is cited?

_____

_____

Step 2   In the Citation Index, look up the feminist poet and philosopher Susan Griffin. (Hint: *AHCI* just uses last name and first and middle initials). Are there any entries for her?_____ If not, look in another recent Citation Index. Under the entry for her name, there will be an item in bold print. This is the name of the book or journal which was cited, it's year of publication, and if it is a journal, the page number of the article. Directly under this, slightly indented in regular type is the name of the author who cited this work, an abbreviated title and volume of the journal in which his or her article appeared, the page number of the article, and the year of publication. There may be additional entries under Griffin in this format. Write down the name of the first person listed who cited Griffin, the journal abbreviation, volume, page number and year here.

_____

_____

Now, look in the front of *AHCI* and find the list of abbreviated journal titles. Write the full name of the journal.

_____

Go to the volume for the same time period which says "Source/Corporate Index" at the top of the spine. Look up the name of the author that you just wrote down. Make a note about a few of the additional elements of information that are provided under the source index entry.

_____   _____

_____   _____

Write down the title of the article below.

_____

_____

Step 3   Find the paper version of *The Philosopher's Index*. Look in the volume(s) of *The Philosopher's Index* that falls in the same and/or the following year as the publication date of your article from *AHCI*. Does the journal listing in the front of the volume indicate that *Hypatia* is indexed here?_____

Is the journal which carried the above article indexed by *The Philosopher's Index*?_____ If so, look in the back half of the index to see if you can find a reference to the article under the author's name.

Did you find it?_____
What types of information are provided by *The Philosopher's Index* that aren't provided by *AHCI* (if you didn't find the article or if the journal is not indexed here, look at any entry under an author in the back to get this information)?

_____

_____

Briefly jot down some of the advantages and disadvantages of *AHCI* and *The Philosopher's Index*.

AHCI   ***Philosopher's Index***

Please hand in this exercise sheet, along with your notes or prints, to your instructor!

Library Research Exercise

Find materials on the role of women in the religions of India.

Step 1   Go to *Women's Studies Abstracts* and select a recent bound volume. Look in the front of the volume for a list of journals covered.

How many journal titles are indexed?_____

Do you notice any trends in the types of journals indexed in *Women's Studies Abstracts*?_____ If so, write them down here.

_____

_____

_____

Step 2   The back of each volume should have a cumulative index for all of the issues in that volume. Look in the index under the subject "India."

Do the subjects have subdivisions?_____

If so, write down an appropriate subdivision for this topic. (Hint: If you can't find a subdivision appropriate to religion, pick another aspect of Indian society for this part of the exercise.)

_____

Look at the number(s) listed next to your subject. These represent the "abstract numbers" not the page number. Write down the first abstract number for your topic._____

Step 3   Turn to the preceding abstract number in the first part of the volume. Write the full citation, including author's name, title of article, and title, volume, issue and page numbers of the journal.

_____

_____

What additional type of information, if any, is provided about this article?

_____

_____

Step 4   Now, find the publication *Studies on Women's Abstracts* and pick a recent bound volume. In this index, the journal listing is found near the back of the volume. Look toward the back and find the listing of journals indexed. Do you notice any differences in the types of materials indexed here and those indexed in *Women's Studies Abstracts*? If so, write them here.

_____

_____

_____

_____

Which is a more comprehensive multidisciplinary index for women's studies?

_____

Step 5   Look at the cumulative subject index in the back of the volume. Once again, look under "India." Do you notice any difference in the quality or completeness of indexing? If so, write down what you found different.

_____

_____

_____

Step 6   Use the abstract numbers to the right of the subject(s) to try to find articles on the topic of Indian religions.

Did you encounter any frustrations or difficulties?_____
If so, please describe them here.

_____

_____

If you find an article on this topic, write down the citation. If you don't, write down the citation for any article dealing with Indian women.

_____

_____

_____

Note that *Studies on Women's Abstracts* includes citations to chapters in books, as well as journal articles.

Please hand in this exercise sheet, along with your notes or prints, to your instructor!

Library Research Exercise

Find biographical information on Mary Elizabeth Bowser, an African-American woman who served as a spy for the Union during the United States Civil War.

Step 1   Go to the on-line catalog. Search for books about Mary Elizabeth Bowser by using her name as a subject search.

Did you find any books about her?_____

If so, print or write down the citation and call number and proceed to Step 2.

_____

_____

_____

Sometimes, if you can't find a book about a person, a book on a broader topic will include information about them. Conduct a keyword search on the terms "women spies" and "civil war." Print or write down the citation and call number for one of these books.

_____

_____

To determine whether this book will have any useful information, you would have to retrieve it from the stacks and examine it.

Step 2   Try a specialized encyclopedia. Often, encyclopedias on a certain topic will have information on elusive personalities. There are many encyclopedias devoted to the civil war. Do a keyword search in the on-line catalog on the terms "encyclopedias" and "civil war" to find call numbers for such encyclopedias in the library, or try the titles which follow:

Faust, Patricia, ed. *Historical Times Illustrated Encyclopedia of the Civil War.* New York: Harper & Row, 1986.

Simmons, Henry Eugene. *A Concise Encyclopedia of the Civil War.* New York: A.S. Barnes, 1965.

Find one of the Civil War encyclopedias in the reference collection. Does it have any information about Mary Elizabeth Bowser?_____ (Hint: If you don't find an entry about her, be sure to check the alphabetical index at the back of the Encyclopedia to see if her information might be in a related article.) If you find an article about her, please make a note about what kind of information it includes.

_____

_____

Step 3   Biographical dictionaries sometimes have brief entries about the lives of notable people. *Biography and Genealogy Master Index (BGMI)* is available in paper copy and CD-ROM and is a valuable general index to biographical dictionaries. Go to *BGMI* in CD-ROM (easier to use) or paper, and look up Bowser's name. Did you find any entries for her?_____ If so, write down the **full title** of a source where you can find information about her. (Hint: To find full titles in the paper version, look up the abbreviation next to the person's name in the front of the volume.)

_____

Also, there are specific indexes to biographical information on women, which cover more obscure sources than *BGMI.* Use the on-line catalog to find the book *Women in Particular: An Index to American Women*, Oryx Press, 1984. Find this book in the reference collection, and look up Bowser's name in the alphabetical index at the back of the book.

To the right of the bold numeral **I**, indicating the first section of the book, there are two numbers. These correspond to the numerical entry number, not the page number. Turn to the first entry number listed for Bowser, and write down the abbreviation you find on the last line of Bowser's entry._____

Now, turn to the front of the book and find the "Source List." Look up the above abbreviation in this list. Write the full title of the source here.

_____

Step 4   Check the on-line catalog to see if the library has a copy of the book noted on the above line. If so, print or write the location and call number.

_____

Go to shelf where this book is located. Look at the entry for Bowser and make a few notes about the kind of information that is contained in this book.

_____

_____

_____

_____

Please hand in this exercise sheet, along with your notes or prints, to your instructor!

NOTES:

Group Activities for Up to 6 Students

This section contains:

Broad Topics; Ways to Focus an Unmanageable Topic in English
Composition
Sarah Brick Archer

Student Self-Teaching of Basic Reference Sources in Freshman English
Composition
Sarah Brick Archer

"And You Are There:" Having Fun with Historical Topics
Sarah Brick Archer

Literary Criticism on William Faulkner
Sarah Brick Archer

"Meeting the Author:" Biographical and Critical Resources on Children's
Literature
Mary Ellen Collins

The Library Beat: How to Find Journalism Sources
Sarah Brick Archer

NOTES:

Broad Topics: Ways to Focus an Unmanageable Topic in English Composition

SARAH BRICK ARCHER

Assistant Professor of Library Services
NORTHEASTERN STATE UNIVERSITY, TAHLEQUAH, OK

Circumstances for the Instruction Session:

This instruction has been useful for Freshman English Composition classes. For this particular class, the English professor requires students to select topics from a list that he has prepared. These are broad subjects and must be narrowed for the term papers. The professor specifically requests that magazines and newspapers be discussed. Several of the professor's topics are used as examples in the class. Five sample group exercises are included in this chapter.

The instruction sessions last for 50 minutes and include approximately 30 students.

Objectives of the Instruction:

- Reduce library anxiety.
- Insure that students understand the basic layout of the library and the services available.
- Teach the concepts of selecting and narrowing a topic.
- Teach the concept of developing a search strategy.
- Introduce the concept of Boolean logic.
- Instruct students how to locate subjects in newspapers and magazines.
- Provide a hands-on group activity to reinforce some of the concepts taught in class.

Components of the Library Instruction:

Part 1 Preparation:

Before class, arrange the room to create the groups. Give each group an exercise. Test all audio visual equipment. Have copies of the *New York Times Index* available for each student. If available, demonstrate any relevant CD-ROM products.

Part 2 Presentation:

- Select an example from one of the professor's broad topics and talk about ways to narrow it. Use a chart on the board, as shown below, with slots for geographic area, time span, interest groups, and perspective. (This chart is based on the one designed and used by Cerise Oberman in the 1987 ACRL Continuing Education Program, *Active Teaching and Learning; A Practical Design Workshop*, Appendix B.)

  Use the broad subject VIOLENCE as the example and show how you would narrow the topic using the chart.

GEOGRAPHIC AREA	TIME SPAN	INTEREST GROUPS	PERSPECTIVE

- Mention specialized encyclopedias and *Library of Congress Subject Headings* for assistance in narrowing topics.

- Discuss the types of materials available in the library and why you would use each kind.

- Discuss how you would locate subjects in magazines and newspapers and where these tools are located.

- While demonstrating indexes, discuss Boolean logic using Venn diagrams.

- Summarize by explaining how you would use the materials to develop a search strategy.

Evaluation:

Be certain to check with each group as it works in the library to ascertain how it is functioning.

Check the exercises to determine if the questions were self explanatory.

Ask the classroom instructor for comments after the instruction session.

Query the students at the end of class to find out if the session seemed helpful.

For a more thorough examination of the session, a survey may be given to the students. This may be done immediately after the session or at the end of the semester after they have applied the concepts that have been taught.

Library Research Exercise

Your broad topic is computer crime.

As you use the indexes, look for ways to narrow your topic. Answer the questions which are listed below:

Step 1   Locate information on your topic in a newspaper.

Newspaper:_____

Date:_____

Page(s):_____

Section:_____

Column:_____

Index used:_____

Step 2   Locate information on your topic in a magazine.

Title of article:_____

_____

Author (if given):_____

Name of magazine:_____

Volume:_____Page(s):_____Date:_____

Step 3   Does the library own the magazine?_____Yes_____No

If owned, what is the call number?_____

Microfilm:_____Shelf:_____Electronic:_____

Index used:_____

Step 4   After using the different indexes, name several different ways that you could narrow your topic.

Step 5   Create a search strategy listing the types of resources that you could consult and the tools that you would use. One example is listed below:

TYPE OF RESOURCE	TOOL
magazine	*Readers' Guide* on CD-ROM

Library Research Exercise

Your broad topic is sexual harassment

As you use the indexes, look for ways to narrow your topic. Answer the following questions:

Step 1   Locate information on your topic in a newspaper.

       Newspaper:_____

       Date:_____

       Page(s):_____

       Section:_____

       Column:_____

       Index used:_____

Step 2   Locate information on your topic in a magazine.

       Title of article:_____

       _____

       Author (if given):_____

       Name of magazine:_____

       Volume:_____Page(s):_____Date:_____

Step 3   Does the library own the magazine?_____Yes_____No

If owned, what is the call number?_____

Microfilm:_____Shelf:_____Electronic:_____

Index used:_____

Step 4   After using the different indexes, name several different ways that you could narrow your topic.

Step 5   Create a search strategy listing the types of resources that you could consult and the tools that you would use. One example is listed below:

TYPE OF RESOURCE	TOOL
magazine	*Readers' Guide* on CD-ROM

Library Research Exercise

Your broad topic is homelessness

As you use the indexes, look for ways to narrow your topic. Answer the following questions:

Step 1   Locate information on your topic in a newspaper.

Newspaper:_____

Date:_____

Page(s):_____

Section:_____

Column:_____

Index used:_____

Step 2   Locate information on your topic in a magazine.

Title of article:_____

_____

Author (if given):_____

Name of magazine:_____

Volume:_____Page(s):_____Date:_____

Step 3   Does the library own the magazine?_____Yes_____No

If owned, what is the call number?_____

Microfilm:_____Shelf:_____Electronic:_____

Index used:_____

Step 4   After using the different indexes, name several different ways that you could narrow your topic.

Step 5   Create a search strategy listing the types of resources that you could consult and the tools that you would use. One example is listed below:

TYPE OF RESOURCE	TOOL
magazine	*Readers' Guide* on CD-ROM

Library Research Exercise

Your broad topic is illegal aliens.

As you use the indexes, look for ways to narrow your topic. Answer the following questions:

Step 1   Locate information on your topic in a newspaper.

Newspaper:_____

Date:_____

Page(s):_____

Section:_____

Column:_____

Index used:_____

Step 2   Locate information on your topic in a magazine.

Title of article:_____

_____

Author (if given):_____

Name of magazine:_____

Volume:_____Page(s):_____Date:_____

Step 3   Does the library own the magazine?_____Yes_____No

If owned, what is the call number?_____

Microfilm:_____Shelf:_____Electronic:_____

Index used:_____

Step 4   After using the different indexes, name several different ways that you could narrow your topic.

Step 5   Create a search strategy listing the types of resources that you could consult and the tools that you would use. One example is listed below:

TYPE OF RESOURCE	TOOL
magazine	*Readers' Guide* on CD-ROM

Library Research Exercise

Your broad topic is child abuse.

As you use the indexes, look for ways to narrow your topic. Answer the following questions:

Step 1   Locate information on your topic in a newspaper.

       Newspaper:_____

       Date:_____

       Page(s):_____

       Section:_____

       Column:_____

       Index used:_____

Step 2   Locate information on your topic in a magazine.

       Title of article:_____

       _____

       Author (if given):_____

       Name of magazine:_____

       Volume:_____Page(s):_____Date:_____

Step 3   Does the library own the magazine?_____Yes_____No

If owned, what is the call number?_____

Microfilm:_____Shelf:_____Electronic:_____

Index used:_____

Step 4   After using the different indexes, name several different ways that you could narrow your topic.

Step 5   Create a search strategy listing the types of resources that you could consult and the tools that you would use. One example is listed below:

TYPE OF RESOURCE	TOOL
magazine	*Readers' Guide* on CD-ROM

NOTES:

Student Self-Teaching of Basic Reference Sources in Freshman English Composition

SARAH BRICK ARCHER

Assistant Professor of Library Services
NORTHEASTERN STATE UNIVERSITY, TAHLEQUAH, OK

Circumstances for the Instruction Session:

This instruction session is designed as an introduction to the library for Freshman English Composition students. Instead of lecturing to students about how to use the various library tools, have the students discover how to use them; then have the students teach the class. (See the section called Hands-on Activity) Sometimes more learning is achieved when students have to teach a subject rather than listen to a lecture.

Most of the work for this type of instructional approach is in preparing for the class, not in teaching it. The teacher's role during the class will be mostly that of facilitator.

The library instruction session lasts for 80 minutes and contains approximately 36 students. For a 50-minute class, you could reduce the number of groups which would shorten the time for presentations. The library instructor could cover the topics not discussed by the groups.

Objectives of the Library Instruction:

- Reduce library anxiety.
- Identify the basic layout of the library and its services.
- Emphasize how and where to get assistance.
- Discuss briefly how to select and narrow a topic.
- Provide hands-on group activities in which students learn how to use

    the on-line catalog,
    specialized encyclopedias,
    a reference book,
    the *Readers' Guide to Periodical Literature*,
    specialized indexes, and
    The New York Times Index.

Components of the Library Instruction:

Part 1   Preparation:

Before class, arrange the tables in the room to create six groups; test all audio visual equipment, and place an exercise, plus any necessary supporting documentation, at each table.

Part 2   Presentation: (approximately 10 minutes)

- Introduce yourself and explain the purpose of the class.
- Provide a brief overview of the layout and services of the library.
- Discuss how to select and narrow a topic.

Hands-on Activity: (approximately 40–60 minutes)

The room should be arranged to define the groups, such as using each table to delineate a group. Each group should have no more than six members. Each group will be researching a different library tool in the search process. The instructor can cover the *New York Times Index*. Be sure to have copies of superseded indexes on the tables. The index exercises were designed to be used with paper indexes, but CD-ROM products could be substituted.

Explain to students that they are to work together in groups to complete the exercise which is to be given to the library instructor. Be certain to tell the students the amount of time given for the exercise (about 15–20 minutes), and that they will be responsible for teaching their classmates. You may shorten this time if you notice the groups breaking down into conversational discussions.

Each group is to choose a recorder to write the answers on the exercise sheet and someone to make the presentation in class. Group members are to help each other. For instance, if a group member has never used the on-line catalog, that individual should use it while the other group members provide support. Explain to the class that the **process** of finding the answer is more important than finding the correct answer.

Explain the relevance of the assignment by stating that this process can be used to research any topic. Tell the students that you will be available for assistance and that they should use any point-of-use instruction that you have provided at their tables. Provide copies of the actual books and indexes for the groups. Walk among the groups to help them get started and to insure that they understand what is expected of them.

Even though the exercises are not to be graded, the students should write their names on the exercise sheet. This might encourage them to take the exercise more seriously.

Allow about 30–40 minutes for the group presentations. One pitfall to this approach is that you might have to correct misinformation that the groups present. This has to be done delicately.

The groups should make their presentations in the following order:

- on-line catalog for books,
- specialized encyclopedia,
- reference books,
- *Readers' Guide to Periodical Literature*,
- on-line catalog for periodicals (if it is not the same as for books)
- specialized index, and
- librarian's presentation on the *New York Times Index*.

Have an LCD panel and overhead projector available so that the groups can demonstrate the indexes or on-line catalog. As each group presents, write the following on the board:

Library Search Strategy:

SOURCE	TOOL
books	on-line catalog
magazines	*Readers' Guide* (or other index)
journals	*Social Sciences Index* (or other index)
newspapers	*New York Times Index*

Follow-up: (approximately 10 minutes)

Explain that all of the sources mentioned can be used to create a search strategy useful in researching any topic. If time permits, try another topic, and based on the sources listed on the board, create a search strategy. If time is available at the end of the class period, show the students where the tools that were discussed in class are located.

Evaluation:

Be certain to check with each group as it works in the library to ascertain how it is functioning.

Check the exercises to determine if the questions were self explanatory.

Ask the classroom instructor for comments after the instruction session.

Query the students at the end of class to determine if the session seemed helpful.

For a more thorough examination of the session, a survey may be given to the students. This could be done immediately after the session or at the end of the semester when they have applied the concepts that have been taught.

Library Research Exercise

Specialized Encyclopedia

*Explain how to find information in the **McGraw-Hill Encyclopedia of Science and Technology**. Locate information on genetic screening for the purposes of this activity.*

Step 1   Why would you use a specialized encyclopedia?

Step 2   At what point in the research process would a specialized encyclopedia be helpful?

Step 3   How would an article in a specialized encyclopedia differ from one in the *World Book*?

Step 4   Is there an index available with the encyclopedia?

Why would you use it?

Step 5   Are there references at the end of the article?

How would they be helpful?

Step 6   How would you ascertain whether the library had the cited sources?

Step 7   How would you locate the *McGraw-Hill Encyclopedia of Science and Technology* in the library?

Library Research Exercise

On-line Catalog

Demonstrate how to use the on-line catalog to locate books. You will be using the computer in the classroom to demonstrate to the class. Include the following items in your discussion:

Step1   Demonstrate how to do a subject search.

Step 2   What is a "line number?"

Step 3   How can you tell how many books there are on a subject?

Step 4   Explain how to determine where books are located and if they are available.

Step 5   Explain what "PS" and "NS" mean?

Step 6   How do you get a "help" screen?

Step 7   What are the commands for author and title searches?

Library Research Exercise

Reference Book

Explain how to find literary criticism on a specific work. For this exercise, use George Orwell's **1984**.

Step 1   Why would you use *Magill's Bibliography of Literary Criticism*?

Step 2   How do you locate the list of criticism available on George Orwell's *1984*?

Step 3   Does the list of criticisms on *1984* include both books and periodicals?_____Yes_____No

How can you distinguish between the sources in books and the ones in periodicals?

Step 4   How would you locate the books and journals in the library?

Step 5   What would you do if the sources were not available in the library?

Step 6   How would you locate *Magill's Bibliography of Literary Criticism* in the library?

Library Research Exercise

Readers' Guide to Periodical Literature

(Hint: If using a print index, look in the front and back of the index for information on how to use it. For the CD-ROM version, examine the help screens.)

*Explain how to locate a subject in the **Readers' Guide**. Have the class participate in your presentation by using their own copies, or CD-ROM version, of the Readers' Guide. Include the following items in your discussion:*

Step 1   Why would you use the *Readers' Guide*?

Step 2   What does it index?

    Books?_____

    Journals?_____

    Newspapers?_____

    Magazines?_____

Step 3   How is it organized?

Step 4   What are cross references? How do you use them?

Step 5   Explain what a sample entry means by identifying each component of an entry.
          (Hint: There should be a sample entry in the index that labels each part, such
          as volume, author, etc.)

Step 6   How do you determine the full title of the periodical in the paper index?

Step 7   How do you find the periodical in the library?

Step 8   Where would you locate the *Readers' Guide* in the library?

Library Research Exercise

Index

(Hint: If using a print index, look in the front or back of the index for information on how to use it. For the CD-ROM version, examine the help screens.)

*Explain how to locate a subject in the **Social Sciences Index**. Include the following items in your discussion.*

Step 1   Why would you use the *Social Sciences Index*?

Step 2   What does it index?

        Books?_____

        Journals?_____

        Newspapers?_____

        Magazines?_____

Step 3   Why would you use the *Social Sciences Index* instead of the *Readers' Guide*?

Step 4 How is it organized?

Step 5 Explain what a sample entry means by identifying each component of an entry. (Hint: There should be a sample entry in the index that labels each part, such as the volume, author, etc.)

Step 6 How do you determine the full title of the periodical in the print index?

Step 7 How do you find the periodical in the library?

Step 8 Where would you locate the *Social Sciences Index* in the library?

Library Research Exercise

On-line Catalog for Periodicals

Using the on-line catalog, demonstrate how to locate periodical holdings information.

Step 1   Why do you have to use the on-line catalog to locate periodical titles?

Step 2   Do you search for the titles of articles or the titles of the periodicals?

Step 3   Use the computer in the classroom to search for a magazine like *Time*. Explain each step that you take, discuss line numbers, holding screens, etc.

Step 4   Explain the holdings screen.

Step 5   Where are periodicals located?

How can you tell if the periodical is on microform, on the shelf in bound volumes, or in electronic format?

"And You Are There:" Having Fun with Historical Topics*

SARAH BRICK ARCHER

Assistant Professor of Library Services
NORTHEASTERN STATE UNIVERSITY, TAHLEQUAH, OK

Circumstances for the Instruction Session:

An English instructor requests library instruction for her second-semester Freshman English Composition class. The English instructor assigns each student a year or range of years between 1940 to 1970. The student must select a topic and research the subject. The library instruction session lasts for one 50-minute class period; the classes contain approximately 30 students.

* "And You Are There" was the title of a newscast presented by Walter Cronkite. The newscast recreated historical events and reported them as if they were currently happening.

Objectives of the Instruction:

- Reduce library anxiety

- Provide general library instruction geared specifically toward the students' assignment.

- Insure that students understand:
    - the basic layout of the library,
    - how to check out materials,
    - the library hours, and
    - where to ask questions.

- Provide general library instruction geared specifically toward the students' assignment:

    1. Introduce chronology reference books,

    2. Demonstrate the on-line catalog using subject headings relevant to the students' library assignment,

    3. Familiarize students with the *Readers' Guide to Periodical Literature*,

    4. Acquaint students with the *New York Times Index*.

Components of the Library Instruction:

Part 1 Preparation:

Before class begins, arrange the room to create six groups. Give an exercise to each group. Write the names and call numbers of some chronologies on the blackboard.

Examples include:
- *The Encyclopedia of American Facts and Dates,*
- *The New York Public Library Book of Chronologies*, and
- *The USA: A Chronicle in Pictures*

Draw a time line from 1940 to the present on the blackboard.

Bring several chronologies to show the class. For each group, have individual copies of the *Readers' Guide* and the *New York Times Index* for hands-on activities.

On a table near the front of the room, have an old microphone and station call letters on a sign to create the setting for a newscast. Include a chair at the table and your script near the microphone.

Part 2 Presentation:

- Identify the purpose of the class which is to discuss how to use the library to research the students' assignments dealing with events that occurred between 1940 and 1970. The lecture and demonstration component should take approximately 35 minutes. Allow at least 10 minutes, preferably 15, for the group exercises.

- For disequilibrium, ask them to play along with you as you pretend to do a Walter Cronkite newscast. You may explain that Walter Cronkite was a newscaster who did a program called "And You Are There" which depicted historical events as if they were currently happening. If this seems too cumbersome, simply choose a current newscaster as an example.

- Sit in front of the microphone and read a series of events that occurred during a specific year and ask the question "and you are there; do you know what year it was?" after each event. The script for the news report contains only a few dates on a page, so that the pages can be turned to imitate a newscaster during a broadcast. Continue to do this until someone guesses the year. The last event should be easy to guess, but if the class does not guess the year, reveal it.

- Use this approach as a lead-in for discussing how to find events that occurred during a specific year. Explain how chronologies can be used to find events that happened during a certain year just as was done with the newscast.

- Use the time line on the blackboard to discuss the types of resources available for their research. Newspapers and magazines for the year in which the event occurred and books written more recently also can discuss the year being studied. Mention the attributes of each type of resource. For instance, the newspapers and magazines provide an emotional eyewitness account while recent books can show trends and how the event affected history.

- Inform the students that they will be applying the information taught during the session by completing group activities.

- Assess the need for any general descriptions about the library, its physical layout, or services.

- Demonstrate the on-line catalog using relevant subject headings. (Example: United States--history--1945--)

- Mention the need for controlled subject headings.

- Remind students that computerized forms of indexes can not be used because they are too recent.

- Have the students use the *Readers' Guide to Periodical Literature* at their tables, as you explain how to use it.

- Demonstrate how to locate a periodical in the library.

- Have the students use the *New York Times Index* at their tables, as you explain how to use it.

- Have the students work in groups to complete the hands-on exercises. Explain how and why they are doing the exercise, and that they are to return to the class when finished. Ask students to write their names on the exercises and turn them in to you.

- Reinforce the concept that the exercise is a microcosm of their future project, and the concepts can be used for other classroom assignments.

- Summarize the session by asking students how they would get started. Write the search strategy on the board.

- Throughout the session, ask for questions, including any general questions about the library.

Evaluation:

Be certain to check with each group as it works in the library to ascertain how it is functioning.

Check the exercises to determine if the questions were self explanatory.

Ask the classroom instructor for comments after the instruction session.

Query the students at the end of class to determine if the session seemed helpful.

For a more thorough examination of the session, a survey may be given to the students. This may be done immediately after the session or at the end of the semester after they have applied the concepts that have been taught.

NEWS REPORT

January 17

The largest federal budget to date has proposed over 98 billion dollars with a proposed 11 billion deficit.

February 21

Medicare, a medical hospital insurance plan financed through Social Security, was submitted to Congress by the president.

April 8

The movie, *Lawrence of Arabia*, won the Academy Award for Best Picture.

April 25

Edward Albee received the Tony award for *Who's Afraid of Virginia Woolf?*

May 15

Grammy award for best group went to Peter, Paul, & Mary. Tony Bennett was a big winner, too.

June 8

The American Heart Association started a drive against cigarettes. They were the first organization to do so.

June 12

Cleopatra, with Richard Burton & Elizabeth Taylor, opened. It was the most expensive picture to date and cost 37 million dollars.

July 21

Jack Nicklaus won the PGA Golf Tournament.

August 28

Freedom March on Washington, DC. Martin Luther King, Jr. presents his speech, "I have a Dream."

November 22

The president was assassinated.

The year is 1963

Library Research Exercise

Harper Lee's 1960 book *To Kill a Mockingbird* won the Pulitzer Prize in 1961.

Your group is going to research this book.

Step 1   Find a book review using the ***Book Review Digest***.

A. Do all the critics agree that *To Kill a Mockingbird* was a good book?

_____

B. Find one periodical that the library owns which reviews the book. Answer the questions below.

What is the title of the magazine?_____

What is the volume number?_____

What is the date?_____

What are the page(s)?_____

What is the call number?_____

Is it on microform, on the shelf, or in electronic format?

_____microform_____shelf_____electronic

Step 2   Find a copy of the book in the library.

A. What is the call number of the book?

_____

B. Where is it located?_____

Step 3   Name one other resource that might help you find information on your topic.

_____

_____

Library Research Exercise

In 1954, Mildred Babe Didrikon Zaharias won the U.S. Women's Open Golf Tournament.

Your group is going to research this event.

Step 1   Use the on-line catalog to locate one book on your subject.

      A. What is the title of the book?

      _____

      _____

      B. Where is it located?

         floor?_____

         call number?_____

Step 2   Locate a magazine article on your subject that the library owns.

      A. What is the title of the magazine?

      _____

      B. What is the volume number?_____

      C. What is the date?_____

      D. What are the page(s)?_____

      E. What is the call number?_____

F. Is it on microform, on the shelf, or in electronic format?

_____microform_____shelf_____electronic

Step 3   Name one other resource that might help you with your research.

_____

_____

Library Research Exercise

This group is doing a paper on an event that happened in 1973.

Set up a search strategy to research the topic by completing the following steps.

Step 1   Use the ***Encyclopedia of American Facts and Dates*** to locate a major event that occurred in 1973.

What is your event?_____

_____

Step 2   Use the on-line catalog to locate one book on your subject.

A. What is the title of the book?

_____

_____

B. Where is it located?

floor?_____

call number?_____

Step 3   Name one other resource that might help you find information on your topic.

_____

_____

Library Research Exercise

This group is doing a paper on the Korean War.

Set up a search strategy to research the topic by completing the following steps.

Step 1   Use the on-line catalog to locate one book on your subject.

   A. What is the title of the book?

   _____

   _____

   B. Where is it located?

   floor?_____

   call number?_____

Step 2   Locate a magazine article on your subject that the library owns.

   A. What is the title of the magazine?

   _____

   B. What is the volume number?_____

   C. What is the date?_____

D. What are the page(s)?_____

E. What is the call number?_____

F. Is it on microform, on the shelf, or in electronic format?

_____microform_____shelf_____electronic

Step 3   Name one other resource that might help you with your research.

_____

_____

Library Research Exercise

This group is doing a paper on the original Woodstock in 1969.

Set up a search strategy to research the topic and include the following items.

Step 1   Locate a magazine article on your subject that the library owns.

     A. What is the title of the magazine?

        _____

     B. What is the volume number?_____

     C. What is the date?_____

     D. What are the page(s)?_____

     E. What is the call number?_____

     F. Is it on microform, on the shelf, or in electronic format?

        _____microform_____shelf_____electronic

Step 2   Locate a newspaper article on your topic.

     A. Name the newspaper_____

        Date_____

        Section_____

        Page_____

        Column_____

Step 3   Name one other resource that might help you find information on the topic.

_____

_____

Step 4   How would you locate information on the second Woodstock that occurred recently?

Use the space below for your answers.

Library Research Exercise

This group is doing a paper on Dr. Jonas Salk's announcement in 1955 of a polio vaccine.

Set up a search strategy to research the topic and include at least three different types of resources. **(Hint: One type would be books.)**

Poliomyelitis may be used as a subject heading. Please list the names and locations of all items found.

Item 1 _____

_____

_____

Item 2 _____

_____

_____

Item 3 _____

_____

_____

Item 4 _____

_____

_____

Item 5 _____

_____

_____

Item 6 _____

_____

_____

Literary Criticism on William Faulkner

SARAH BRICK ARCHER

Assistant Professor of Library Services
NORTHEASTERN STATE UNIVERSITY, TAHLEQUAH, OK

Circumstances for the Instruction Session:

This instruction session is taught for an upper division English class on William Faulkner. Student projects involve locating literary criticism on Faulkner's works and biographical information on the author. The library instruction session consists of one 50-minute session for approximately 20 students.

Objectives of the Instruction:

- Reduce library anxiety.

- Teach the students how to locate biographical and general information about William Faulkner.

- Instruct the student how to find criticism on specific works of William Faulkner.

- Assist the students in learning how to develop a search strategy.

- Provide a hands-on group activity in which the students apply the skills delineated in objectives 2 and 3.

Components of the Library Instruction:

Part 1   Preparation:

Before class, arrange the room to create three groups. Test all audio visual equipment. Bring examples of reference books and periodicals to the class. Give an exercise to each group.

Part 2 Presentation: (approximately 30 minutes)

- To begin the class, read an excerpt from one of Faulkner's short stories and an excerpt from a corresponding criticism on the same work. Use this to generate a discussion about why students would want to locate literary criticism.

- Explain that the purpose of the class is to help the students efficiently locate criticism. Refer students to the handout which contains a list of materials that will be discussed during class. The handout will be found following the student activities.

- Structure a class presentation around the need to create a search strategy. Discuss the attributes of different library materials and what role they would play in developing a search strategy.

- Use the on-line catalog with an LCD panel and overhead projector (or, if in an electronic classroom, load the catalog on each workstation) to demonstrate the on-line catalog, *Humanities Index*, *M.L.A. Bibliography*, and any other relevant indexes on CD-ROM.

- Discuss the usefulness of such reference tools as literary explicators, specialized Faulkner indexes, Faulkner glossaries, bibliographies, etc. Mention the *Faulkner Journal* and other useful literary journals.

Hands-on Activity: (approximately 10 minutes)

The room should be arranged to define the groups, such as using tables to delineate them. Each group should have no more than six members and will be researching a different Faulkner work. Explain to students that they are to work together in groups to complete the exercise which is to be given to the library instructor at the end of the class period.

Each group is to choose a recorder to write the answers on the exercise sheet. Group members are to help each other. For instance, if a group member has never used the on-line catalog, that individual should search the catalog while the other group members provide support. Explain to the class that the process of finding the answer is more important than finding the correct answer.

All reference sources consulted should be listed on the exercise. Encourage the class to use the handout as a guide in selecting a source that might answer the questions. More than one source can be used to find the answer.

Identify the relevance of the assignment to the class by explaining that the exercise reflects what the students will be doing in their class and that the concepts taught will be useful in other English classes. Inform students that you will be in the reference area for questions, and that after they have completed the exercise, they are to return to the classroom to discuss what they have learned.

Even though the exercises are not to be graded, the students should write their names on the exercise sheet. This might encourage them to take the exercise more seriously.

When the students are finished with the exercise, return to the classroom for a follow-up which should last about 10 minutes. Each group should discuss the search strategy that it used and what it discovered. Summarize what was discussed during the class period.

Evaluation:

Be certain to check with each group as it works in the library to ascertain how it is functioning.

Check the exercises to determine if the questions were self explanatory.

Ask the classroom instructor for comments after the instruction session.

Query the students at the end of class to inquire if the session seemed helpful.

For a more thorough examination of the session, a survey may be given to the students. This may be done immediately after the session or at the end of the semester after they have applied the concepts that have been taught.

Library Research Exercise

Your group is going to research William Faulkner's "*Dry September.*"

Step 1   Create a search strategy for researching the literary work "*Dry September*" by William Faulkner.

            List the titles of reference tools that you believe would be useful in locating criticism on "*Dry September.*"

_____

_____

_____

_____

Step 2   Using the tools listed above, locate a periodical article available in this library that critiques "*Dry September.*" Include the following information:

Author_____

Title of article_____

Name of journal_____

Volume number_____

Date_____

Pages_____

Call number_____

Floor location (for print volume)_____

Microfilm_____Electronic_____

Step 3   Using the tools listed in Step 1, locate a section in a book, available in this library, that critiques *"Dry September."*

    Include the following information:

Author of book_____

Title of book_____

Pertinent page(s)_____

Call number of book_____

Step 4   Be prepared to discuss how you used the reference tools and any problems that you encountered.

Library Research Exercise

Your group is going to research William Faulkner's "*Barn Burning*."

Step 1   Create a search strategy for researching this literary work.

List, in the space provided below, the titles of reference tools that you believe would be useful in locating criticism on "*Barn Burning*."

_____

_____

_____

_____

_____

Step 2   Using the tools listed above, locate a periodical article available in this library that critiques "*Barn Burning*." Include the following information:

Author_____

Title of article_____

_____

Name of journal_____

Volume number_____   Date_____

Pages_____   Call number_____

Floor location (print volume)_____   Microfilm_____

Electronic_____

Step 3   Using the tools listed in Step 1, locate a section in a book, available in this library, that critiques *"Barn Burning."* Include the following information:

Author of book_____

Title of book_____

Pertinent page(s)_____

Call number of book_____

Step 4   Be prepared to discuss how you used the reference tools and any problems that you encountered.

Library Research Exercise

Your group is going to research William Faulkner's Light in August.

Step 1   Create a search strategy for researching the literary work *Light in August.*

List the titles of reference tools that you believe would be useful in locating criticism on *Light in August.*

_____

_____

_____

_____

Step 2   Using the tools listed above, locate a periodical article available in this library that critiques *Light in August.* Include the following information:

Author_____

Title of article_____

_____

Name of journal_____

Volume number_____   Date_____

Page(s)_____   Call number_____

Floor location (print volume)_____Microfilm_____

Electronic_____

Step 3   Using the tools listed in Step 1, locate a section in a book available in this library, that critiques *Light in August*. Include the following information:

Author of book_____

Title of book_____

Pertinent page(s)_____

Call number of book_____

Step 4   Be prepared to discuss how you used the reference tools and any problems that you encountered.

Finding Literary Criticism on William Faulkner

How do I know which explicator to use?
Consult the *Literary Criticism Index*
Consult *Literary Research Guide* for guides on reference tools in literature

How do I find general sources on Faulkner?
William Faulkner: A Reference Guide
A Glossary of Faulkner's South
William Faulkner's Characters: An Index to the Published and Unpublished Fiction
WWW
   http://www.mcsr.olemiss.edu/~egjbp/faulkner/faulkner.html

How do I find criticism on Faulkner's short stories?
Masterplots is useful for a quick overview to a short story.
For more in-depth discussions, use the following sources:
American Short-Fiction Criticism & Scholarship
Short Fiction Criticism
Twentieth-Century Short Story Explication

How do I find criticism on Faulkner's novels?
Masterplots is useful for a quick overview to a novel
For more in-depth discussions, use the following sources:
American Novel, 1789–1977: A Checklist of Twentieth Century Criticism
Articles on Twentieth Century Literature: An Annotated Bibliography
Contemporary Novel
Literary Criticism and Authors' Biographies
Magill's Bibliography of Literary Criticism

How do I find brief biographical information about Faulkner?

Dictionary of Literary Biography is good for a quick overview to William Faulkner
For more in-depth information, find books about Faulkner by searching him as a
subject in the on-line catalog.

How do I find periodical articles about Faulkner?

Many of the explicators listed above index periodicals as well as sections within
  books.
Useful indexes to consult include the following:
The Humanities Index (available both in print and on CD-ROM)
M.L.A. Bibliography (available both in print and on CD-ROM)
The Faulkner Journal

How do I find definitions of literary terms?

A Handbook to Literature

Where can I locate an *M.L.A.* style manual?

M.L.A. Handbook for Writers of Research Papers

NOTES:

"Meeting the Author:" Biographical and Critical Resources of Children's Literature

MARY ELLEN COLLINS

Reference Librarian
PURDUE UNIVERSITY LIBRARIES

Circumstances for the Instruction Session:

An instructor from Purdue's School of Education requested a library lecture for her five sections of the course "Media for Children." The library session will be a 50-minute instruction for each of the five sessions. Sources for the eight required written projects will be presented. Emphasis will be on the biographical and critical views of the authors' lives and work. These publications will be listed in the "Children's Literature Pathfinder." Additionally, a scheme of the library's collection of children's books will be distributed and discussed.

There are six library exercises, which can be used with smaller groups of students within a class of thirty or so.

Objectives of the Instruction:

- To instill confidence in students in their use of the library.

- To locate the children's literature books in the library, using a diagram of the collection on the third floor of the library.

- To instruct on the reference tools that students will use to find material for eight writing assignments for the course, one of which is a 6–9 page final paper due the last week of class.

- To show which sources provide book reviews, and which provide literary criticism (or bio-critical articles).

Components of the Library Instruction:

Preparation:

1. Provide copies of the handouts for the class Media for Children; each session has an average of 30 students. The handout "Children's Literature Pathfinder" is appended following the student activities; no call numbers are included so that it will be more useful to other librarians.

2. Collect several titles on the list from the reference collection, place these on a book truck, and take them to class. Students can examine these titles as the librarian discusses each one.

In-class Presentation:

1. Discuss the location/arrangement of the children's book collection.

2. Discuss the bibliography called "Children's Literature Pathfinder." It is divided into the sections listed below:

   - Awards and Prizes
   - Biography
   - Book Reviews/Bibliographies
   - Character Dictionaries
   - Children's Literature—History and Criticism
   - Newbery and Caldecott Speeches
   - Indexes
   - Problem-Centered Books
   - Periodicals Relevant to Children's Literature
   - Children's Literature Web Sites

   Not all sources in the bibliography will be discussed in class. This resource is also one that students can use when they are working in the profession, or on their own, when some of the other sources may be more relevant, e.g., the poetry indexes.

   Note: The identification of Purdue University Libraries and Dewey call numbers have been omitted to make the materials in this book more adaptable for use in other settings.

3. Emphasize the need for students to consult these sources for biographical information: the *Junior Author* series by H. W. Wilson, the latest index for *Something About the Author*, and *Contemporary Authors.*. (*Contemporary Authors* is available in paper and also on CD-ROM). Remind them that *Biography Index* can be helpful in some cases.

4. Emphasize the use of these sources when students need titles for special situations: *Children's Catalog, Best Books for Children* (Gillespie and Naden), *Wordless/Almost Wordless Picture Books* (Richey and Puckett), *A to Zoo: Subject Access to Children's Picture Books* (Lima and Lima). These titles will have subject access that will help students in selecting children's literature books to fit particular curricular needs in social studies, science, or other subjects.

5.   Stress that children's literature criticism involves the use of many of the above materials as well as others especially suited to that purpose. The criticism of children's literature is a growing genre, but material may still be hard for students to find, and many assignments require them to write papers that employ use of principles of literary criticism. Some sources that are pointed out in this library lecture are from the list given to the students:

A. *Dictionary of Literary Biography*, particularly
   v.22, *American Writers for Children, 1900–1960*;
   v.42, *American Writers for Children Before 1900*;
   v.52, *American Writers for Children Since 1960*;
   v.61, *American Writers for Children Since 1960: Poets, Illustrators, and Non*
          Fiction Writers;
   v.141, *British Children's Writers 1880–1914*.

B. *Writers for Children* (Bingham)
   This title contains 84 bio-critical essays, each on a noted children's author/illustrator, written by scholars in the field. These essays include deceased authors only.

C. *Children's Literature Review*
   Published about twice a year, each volume covers several authors whose work is treated as a corpus, then each individual work is discussed, accompanied by summaries of articles/book reviews which have the full citation following.

D. *Newbery and Caldecott Medalists and Honor Book Winners: Bibliographies and Resource Material Through 1991*
   This source offers a bibliography of articles and includes essays on each author.

E. *Children's Literature: A Guide to the Criticism* (Hendrickson)
   Although dated, it offers excellent material in articles and book chapters on selected authors, as well as themes, genres and movements in children's literature.

Evaluation:

No formal evaluation has been used for this library lecture. Students are encouraged to come to the library to seek help with their term projects. Since there are many throughout the term, that is the basis on which to build knowledge of library sources. However, the exercises can be used with the class.

Library Exercises:

There are six library exercises that accompany this lecture as follow-up. They can be used with small groups of four to six students per class. The students can meet informally to consult about the sources for use in each exercise, and can decide to select questions to answer individually among themselves within these small groups. The exercises should be turned in to the librarian or to the class professor within two days of the lecture. The librarian and the professor will confer about the results to see what learning occurred.

Library Exercise

This group will examine the three titles described below.

Something About the Author

This source is biographical in the type of information provided. Data include well established and emerging authors and illustrators primarily from English-speaking nations, and others whose work is translated into English. Pictures are plentiful, and a cumulative index is found in every other issue.

Something About the Author: Autobiography Series

This series contains original autobiographical essays written by the authors and illustrators themselves for this publication. These essays represent a first person approach to the writer's or illustrator's life; photographs accompany the essays.

Children's Literature Review

This title is published about twice a year; each volume covers several authors whose work is treated as a corpus in a general discussion. Each work is then discussed, followed by summaries of articles/book reviews, which are accompanied by the citation to the original piece. It provides information itself, and indexes information.

Step 1   Using *Something About the Author*:

In what volumes can you locate essays about William Steig?

_____

Step 2   Using *Children's Literature Review*:

A. Where else would you locate entries about William Steig?

_____

_____

_____

B. Is John Steptoe still living?_____

What are some of the books he wrote and illustrated?

_____

_____

_____

_____

_____

C. For what kind of children's literature is Lloyd Alexander best known?

_____

_____

_____

_____

D. What was a title that he wrote which was not aimed for children?

_____

_____

Step 3   Using *Something About the Author: Autobiography Series*:

A. Find the entry on Beverly Cleary. Describe how this article is different from one that would be found in *Something About the Author*.

_____

_____

B. Would you feel that both are necessary in order to write an insightful paper on her work? _____

Why or why not?

_____

_____

_____

_____

_____

Library Exercise

This group will examine the titles described below.

Children's Literature Review

This title is published about twice a year; each volume covers several authors whose work is treated as a corpus in a general discussion. Each work is then discussed, followed by summaries of articles/book reviews, which are accompanied by the citation to the original piece. It provides information itself, and indexes information.

Children's Literature Awards & Winners: A Directory of Prizes, Authors, and Illustrators

This source lists awards given around the world for children's books, and each winner. The third edition is cumulative, and includes lists of the authors with all awards won, as well as indexes by author/illustrator, title and award.

Step 1 Look up Ellen Raskin in the latest index of *Children's Literature Review*. In what other source can you find information about her?

_____

_____

_____

A. How is the article about Ellen Raskin in vol.12 of this serial arranged, i.e., what components does it have?

_____

_____

_____

B. What award did she win, and when did she win it?

_____

_____

Step 2   Where is Margaret Mahy's home?_____

_____

A. What types of books has she written?

_____

_____

_____

_____

B. Name a nonfiction book written by her_____

_____

C. Did she win any awards?_____What were they?

_____

_____

_____

Step 3   In what sources is Graeme Base's book *Animalia* reviewed?

_____

_____

A. How would you describe this book?

_____

_____

_____

B. Look in *Children's Literature: Awards and Winners* (3rd Ed.) and list the awards Graeme Base won for *Anamalia*.

_____

_____

_____

Library Exercise

This group will examine the titles listed below.

The *Junior Author Series*
This is a series in six volumes that includes essays about authors' lives. These are of medium length, accompanied by a portrait.

Something About the Author
This source is biographical in the type of information provided. Data include well established and emerging authors and illustrators primarily from English-speaking nations, and others whose work is translated into English. Pictures are plentiful, and a cumulative index is found in every other issue.

Children's Literature Review
This title is published about twice a year; each volume covers several authors whose work is treated as a corpus in a general discussion. Each work is then discussed, followed by summaries of articles/book reviews, which are accompanied by the citation to the original piece. It provides information itself, and indexes information.

Step 1   Look up Lynd Ward in the *Junior Author* series and in *Something About the Author*. How do these two entries differ?

_____

_____

_____

A. What type of work did Lynd Ward produce?

_____

B. With whom did Lynd Ward collaborate?_____

Step 2   Look up John Neufeld in *Something About the Author*. What is his birth

date?_____

A. What type of book is *Lisa Bright and Dark*?_____

_____

_____

B. For what audience was this book intended?_____

_____

C. Where has the book been reviewed, as noted in *Something About the*

Author?_____

_____

D. What kind of books does he write?_____

_____

Step 3   Look in *Children's Literature Review* and find an entry about Natalie Babbitt.

How is it arranged?_____

_____

_____

A. What did Eudora Welty say about *KneeKnock Rise*?

_____

_____

_____

B. What type of book was *Goody Hall*?_____

_____

_____

_____

Library Exercise

This group will examine the titles described below.

Something About the Author: Autobiography Series

This series contains original autobiographical essays written by the authors and illustrators themselves for this publication. These essays represent a first person approach to the writer's or illustrator's life. Photographs also accompany these essays.

Children's Literature Review

This title is published about twice a year; each volume covers several authors whose work is treated as a corpus in a general discussion. Each work is then discussed, followed by summaries of articles/book reviews, which are accompanied by the citation to the original piece. It provides information itself, and indexes information.

Step 1   In *Something About the Author: Autobiography Series*, find the article on Jane

Yolen. When was she born?_____

A. What type of material did she write?_____

_____

_____

B. How would you describe her writing career?_____

_____

_____

Step 2   In *Children's Literature Review*, look up Paula Danziger. For what audience

were her books intended?_____

_____

A. Why would *The Cat Ate My Gymsuit* be popular with young people?

_____

B. What sources are noted here as reviewing this book?_____

_____

C. How did Paula Danziger benefit from her teaching experiences as far as
her writing is concerned?

_____

_____

_____

Step 3   In *Children's Literature Review*, look up Arnold Adoff. What were some of his

pursuits?_____

_____

_____

A. What types of literature did he write for children?_____

_____

_____

_____

B. What kind of book is *Black Is Brown Is Tan*?_____

_____

_____

Library Exercise

This group will examine the titles described below.

Something About the Author.

This source is biographical in the type of information provided. Data include well established and emerging authors and illustrators primarily from English-speaking nations, and others whose work is translated into English. Pictures are plentiful, and a cumulative index is found in every other issue.

Children's Literature Review

This title is published about twice a year; each volume covers several authors whose work is treated as a corpus in a general discussion. Each work is then discussed, followed by summaries of articles/book reviews, which are accompanied by the citation to the original piece. It provides information itself, and indexes information.

Step 1   Look up Margaret Hodges and Margaret Mary Kimmel in *Something About the*

Author. What is similar about their careers?_____

_____

_____

A. What kind of writing do they do?_____

_____

_____

B. Look up books by each of these authors in the library. List titles held with

call numbers._____

_____

_____

_____

_____

_____

_____

_____

_____

Step 2   In *Children's Literature Review*, look up Tomie de Paola. What kind of work

does he do?_____

_____

_____

A. What is his background?_____

_____

_____

B. How would you describe *Nana Upstairs and Nana Downstairs*?

_____

_____

Step 3 Look up Susan Cooper in *Children's Literature Review*. What is the setting for

her novels?_____

_____

A. What awards did she win for her books?_____

_____

_____

B. Of what country is she a native?_____

Library Exercise

This group will examine the titles described below.

Children's Literature Review

This title is published about twice a year; each volume covers several authors whose work is treated as a corpus in a general discussion. Each work is then discussed, followed by summaries of articles/book reviews, which are accompanied by the citation to the original piece. It provides information itself, and indexes information.

Writers for Children (Bingham)

This title contains 84 bio-critical essays, each on a noted children's author/illustrator, and written by scholars in the field. These essays include deceased authors only.

Step 1   In *Children's Literature Review* look up Paula Fox. For what novel did she win the Newbery Medal?

_____

A. How does Julius Lester feel about the book as shown in the reprinted review?

_____

_____

B. Does the library have her books? If so, write the titles and call

numbers._____

_____

_____

Step 2   In *Children's Literature Review*, look up Paul Zindel. What kind of writing did he do, in addition to writing for children?

_____

_____

A. What was his first book?_____

_____

B. How would you rate it, given the reviews?_____

_____

Step 3   In Jane Bingham's *Writers for Children*, look up the article on Wanda Gag. How would you describe the tone of this article?

_____

_____

A. How would it help you understand her life and/or her work?_____

_____

B. Who is the author of this article?_____

Children's Literature Pathfinder

Awards and Prizes:

Children's Literature Awards & Winners: A Directory of Prizes, Authors and Illustrators. Dolores Blythe Jones, comp. Detroit: Gale, 1983–

Newbery and Caldecott Awards: A Guide to the Medal and Honor Books. Chicago: American Library Association, Association for Library Service to Children, 1995.

Biography:

Fifth Book of Junior Authors & Illustrators. New York: H.W. Wilson, 1983.

Fourth Book of Junior Authors & Illustrators. New York: H.W. Wilson, 1978.

Fuller, Muriel. *More Junior Authors.* New York: H.W. Wilson, 1963.

Kunitz, Stanley. *The Junior Book of Authors.* 2d ed., rev. N.Y: H.W. Wilson, 1951.

Sixth Book of Junior Authors & Illustrators. New York: H.W. Wilson, 1989.

Something About the Author. Detroit: Gale, 1971–

Something About the Author: Autobiography Series. Detroit: Gale, 1986–

Third Book of Junior Authors. New York: H. W. Wilson, 1972.

Yesterday's Authors of Books for Children. Detroit: Gale, 1977–1978. 2 vols.

Additional Sources for Biographical Information:

Biography Index. New York: H. W. Wilson, 1946–
   Citations refer to biographical dictionaries, books and periodicals.

Contemporary Authors. Detroit: Gale, 1967– *Index* from v.1–
   Also: *Contemporary Authors, New Revision Series,* and *Contemporary Authors, Autobiography Series.*

Book Reviews/Bibliographies:

Children's Book Review Index. Detroit: Gale, 1975–

Children's Catalog. New York: H.W. Wilson, 1991.
(Published quinquennially, plus annual supplements.)

CCBC Choices 1993. Madison, Wisconsin: University of Wisconsin-Madison,
School of Education, Cooperative Children's Book Center, 1994.

*The Elementary School Library Collection: A Guide to Books and other Media,
Phases 1, 2, 3.* 18th Ed. Williamsport, PA.: Brodart Co., 1992.

Gillespie, John T. and Corinne J. Naden. *Best Books for Children: Preschool
Through Grade 6.* Fifth edition. New York: R.R. Bowker, 1994.

Lynn, Ruth Nadelman. *Fantasy Literature for Children and Young Adults: An
Annotated Bibliography.* 4th ed. New York: R.R. Bowker, 1995.

Miller-Lachmann, Lyn. *Our Family, Our Friends, Our World: An Annotated
Guide to Significant Multicultural Books for Children and Teenagers.* New
York: R.R. Bowker, 1991.

Ramirez, Gonzalo. *Multicultural Children's Literature.* Albany, New York:
Delmar Publishers, 1994.

Richey, Virginia H., and Katharyn E. Puckett. *Wordless/Almost Wordless Picture
Books: A Guide.* Englewood, Colorado: Libraries Unlimited, 1992.

Character Dictionaries:

Fisher, Margery Turner. *Who's Who in Children's Books: a Treasury of the
Familiar Characters of Childhood.* New York: Holt, Rinehart and Winston,
1975.

Children's Literature--History and Criticism:

Bingham, Jane M. *Writers for Children: Critical Studies of Major Authors Since the Seventeenth Century.* New York: Charles Scribners Sons, 1988.

Bettelheim, Bruno. *The Uses of Enchantment: the Meaning and Importance of Fairy Tales.* New York: Knopf, 1976.

Children's Literature Review. Detroit: Gale, 1976–

Haviland, Virginia. *Children's Literature: A Guide to Reference Sources.* Washington, D.C.: Library of Congress, 1966.
_____. *Supplement I.* 1972.
_____. *Supplement II.* 1977.

Hazard, Paul. *Books, Children and Men.* 4th ed. Boston: Horn Book, 1963.

Helbig, Alethea K. *Dictionary of Children's Fiction From Australia, Canada, India, New Zealand, and Selected African Countries.* New York: Greenwood Press, 1992.

Hendrickson, Linnea. *Children's Literature: A Guide to the Criticism.* Boston: G. K. Hall, 1987.

Huck, Charlotte S., Susan Hepler, & Janet Hickman. *Children's Literature in the Elementary School.* 5th ed. N.Y.: Harcourt, Brace, Jovanovich, 1993.

MacCann, Donnarae and Gloria Woodard. *The Black American in Books for Children.* 2d ed. Metuchen, N. J.: Scarecrow, 1985.

MacCann, Donnarae. *The Child's First Books: A Critical Study of Pictures and Texts.* New York: H.W. Wilson, 1973.

Meigs, Cornelia Lynde. *A Critical History of Children's Literature.* New York: Macmillan, 1969.

Newbery and Caldecott Medalists and Honor Book Winners: Bibliographies and Resource Material Through 1991. 2d ed. N.Y.: Neal-Schuman Publ., 1992.

Smith, Lillian H. *The Unreluctant Years: A Critical Approach to Children's Literature.* Chicago: American Library Association, 1953.

Sutherland, Zena. *Children and Books.* 8th ed. N.Y.: Harper/Collins, 1991.

The following sources are grouped together, in two distinct groups, because of special format/treatment of the subject matter. These include the Newbery/Caldecott speeches collected in editions by Horn Book, and the bio-critical articles in volumes of the *Dictionary of Literary Biography*. Both groups are valuable for the views that they offer on any given author's or illustrator's work.

Newbery and Caldecott Speeches:

These volumes are listed in chronological order of the speeches included. Later speeches may be found in volumes of the Horn Book Magazine (generally June or August):

Miller, Bertha Mahoney and Elinor Whitney Field. *Newbery Medal Books: 1922–1955*. Boston: Horn Book, 1955.

Miller, Bertha Mahony and Elinor Whitney Field. *Caldecott Medal Books: 1938–1957*. Boston: Horn Book, 1957.

Kingman, Lee. *Newbery and Caldecott Medal Books: 1956–1965*. Boston: Horn Book, 1965.

Kingman, Lee. *Newbery and Caldecott Medal Books: 1966–1975*. Boston: Horn Book, 1975.

Kingman, Lee. *Newbery and Caldecott Medal Books: 1976–1985*. Boston: Horn Book, 1986.

The following volumes of the *Dictionary of Literary Biography* contain bio-critical essays of authors and illustrators in the area of children's literature. They are listed in the order of the volume number:

Dictionary of Literary Biography, vol. 22: American Writers for Children, 1900–1960. Detroit: Gale, 1983.

Dictionary of Literary Biography, vol. 42: American Writers for Children Before 1900. Detroit: Gale, 1985.

Dictionary of Literary Biography, vol. 52: American Writers for Children Since 1960. Detroit: Gale, 1986.

Dictionary of Literary Biography, v. 61: American Writers for Children Since 1960; Poets, Illustrators and Non Fiction Writers. Detroit: Gale, 1987.

Dictionary of Literary Biography, v. 141: British Children's Writers, 1880–1914. Detroit: Gale, 1994.

Children's Literature Journals-Indexes/Lists:

Collins, Mary Ellen. *Education Journal and Serials: An Analytical Guide*. Westport, Connecticut: Greenwood Press, 1988. See entry numbers 399, 407, 409, 417, 491–502, and 786.

International Jugend Bibliothek. *Professional Periodicals in International Children's Literature: A Guide*. Marianne Reetz, comp. Munich, Germany: The Author, 1994.

Indexes:

Brewton, John and Sara Brewton. *Index to Children's Poetry*. New York: H.W. Wilson, 1942.
_____. *Supplement I*. 1954.
_____. *Supplement II*. 1965.

Brewton, John and Sara Brewton. *Index to Poetry for Children and Young People, 1964–69*. New York: H.W. Wilson, 1972.

Brewton, John, Meredith G. Blackburn and Lorraine A. Blackburn. *Index to Poetry for Children and Young People, 197–-1975*. New York: H.W. Wilson, 1978.

Brewton, John, Meredith G. Blackburn and Lorraine A. Blackburn. *Index to Poetry for Children and Young People, 1976–1981*. New York: H.W. Wilson, 1984.

Lima, Carolyn W. and John A. Lima. *A to Zoo: Subject Access to Children's Picture Books*. 3rd. ed. New York: R.R. Bowker, 1989.

Problem Centered Books:

Dryer, Sharon Spredemann. *The Bookfinder: A Guide to Children's Literature About the Needs and Problems of Youth Aged 2–15*. Circle Pines, Minnesota: American Guidance Service, 1977–

Rasinski, Timothy N. and Cindy S. Gillespie. *Sensitive Issues: an Annotated Guide to Children's Literature K–6*. Phoenix, Arizona: Oryx, 1992.

Children's Materials Publishing/For Writers, Illustrators:

Children's Writer's and Illustrator's Market: Where to Sell Your Fiction,
Nonfiction, and Illustrations for Every Age Group—From Toddlers to
Teen. Lisa Carpenter, ed. Cincinnati, Ohio: Writer's Digest Books, 1993.

Periodicals Relevant to Children's Literature:

New Advocate, 1981–1986; New Series, 1987–
Book Links, 1991–
Bookbird, 1963–
Bulletin of the Center for Children's Books, 1947–
Children's Literature: Annual of the Modern Language Association Division on
     Children's Literature and the Children's Literature Association, 1972–
Children's Literature Association Quarterly, 1976–
Children's Literature in Education, 1970–
Five Owls, 1986–
Horn Book Magazine, 1924–
International Review of Children's Literature and Librarianship, 1986–
Language Arts (Preceded by *Elementary English*), 1924–
Lion and the Unicorn, 1977–
School Library Journal, 1954–
Signal, 1970–

Internet Sources for Children's Literature:

• One source for information on aspects of children's literature is the Web site prepared
  by David K. Brown at the University of Calgary.

  The URL is:http://www.ucalgary.ca/~dkbrown/index.html

  This is a broad based approach to children's literature. It contains information on
  resources that teachers and others can use with the literature. Among other items in
  this site are publisher data and children's literature research helps.

• Another source of internet information is *YAHOO* which is also a copyrighted
  website, by Yahoo, Inc., which offers access to many fields by keyword search.
  Some aspects of children's literature covered by *YAHOO* include information on

books for children and young adults, information for persons who are writing children's literature, and book producers. *YAHOO* is a very broad Web index, providing access to a wide array of subjects. It offers initial broad topics, as well as providing the means for users to initiate their own searches.

The URL for *YAHOO* is: http://www.yahoo.com

- *Alta Vista* is another Web index, which provides an entre into the World Wide Web via a subject search. This is a copyrighted index produced by Digital Equipment Corporation. It is broad based in subject approach.

The URL for *Alta Vista* is: http://www.altavista.digital.com/

The Library Beat: How to Find Journalism Sources in the Library

SARAH BRICK ARCHER

Assistant Professor of Library Services
NORTHEASTERN STATE UNIVERSITY, TAHLEQUAH, OK

Circumstances for the Instruction Session:

A Mass Communications instructor requests a library instruction session for her Basic Writing for the Media class in which the students are learning to gather, write, and evaluate news. The class session emphasizes how to find information in the library for a story and how to locate professional journalism materials. The library instruction session lasts for 50 minutes and contains approximately 30 students.

Objectives of the Instruction:

- Reduce library anxiety.
- Insure that students understand the basic layout of the library and its services.
- Introduce the students to specific tools in their discipline, both journalism and tools useful for locating factual information.
- Provide a hands-on group activity in which the students look for factual news items.

Components of the Library Instruction:

Part 1 Preparation:

Before class, arrange the room to create five groups. Give an exercise to each group. Bring examples of reference books and periodicals to the class. Test all audio visual equipment that you plan to use.

Part 2   Presentation: (approximately 30 minutes)

To begin the class, read "In Praise of Libraries," (in *How to Interview: The Art of Asking Questions, by* Paul McLaughlin. North Vancouver, British Columbia: International Self-Council Press, 1990, p. 34-37) to introduce the class to the concept of library research in journalism. If this book is not available, use another source that discusses research in the field of journalism. Use this as an umbrella for your class instruction session.

Explain the purpose of the class, i.e., how to locate journalism materials and information for a story. Refer students to the handout which contains a list of materials that will be discussed during class. This handout will be found following the student activities.

Use the on-line catalog with an LCD panel and overhead projector (or, if in an electronic classroom, load the catalog on each individual PC) to demonstrate how to find books to improve their journalistic style. Some categories to use are as follows:

- serials that show excellent writing

- style manuals

- dictionaries

In locating material for a story, discuss the reference collection and periodicals. Refer to the handout for titles and locations of reference materials. Circulate sample reference books and periodicals. Describe the arrangement of materials and the types of reference sources.

Demonstrate how to use the periodical indexes. Use superseded print indexes or use an LCD panel and overhead projector to demonstrate CD-ROM databases.

Hands-on Activity: (approximately 10 minutes)

Since this is a Mass Communications class, the questions on the exercises should be very current. The exercises can be changed to keep the questions up-to-date.

The room should be arranged to define the groups, such as using tables to delineate the groups. Each group should have no more than six members. Explain to students that they are to work together in groups to complete the exercise which is to be given to the library instructor.

Each group is to choose a recorder to write the answers on the exercise sheet. Group members are to help each other. For instance, if a group member has never used the on-line catalog, that individual should search the catalog while the other group members provide support. Explain to the class that the **process** of finding the answer is more important than finding the correct answer.

All reference sources consulted should be listed on the exercise. Encourage the class to use the bibliography as a guide in selecting a source that might answer the question. More than one source can be used to find the answer.

Identify the relevance of the assignment to the class by explaining that the exercise reflects what the students will be doing in their classes as well as on the job. Tell students that you will be in the reference area for questions, and that after the students have completed the exercise, they are to return to the classroom to discuss what they have learned.

Even though the exercises are not to be graded, the students should write their names on the exercise sheet. This might encourage them to take the exercises more seriously.

When the students are finished with the exercise, return to the classroom and have a follow-up for about 10 minutes. Each group should discuss the search strategy that they used and what they discovered. Summarize what was discussed during the class period.

Evaluation:

Be certain to check with each group as it works in the library to ascertain how it is functioning.

Check the exercises to determine if the questions were self explanatory.

Ask the classroom instructor for comments after the instruction session.

Query the students at the end of class to inquire if the session seemed helpful.

For a more thorough examination of the session, a survey may be given to the students. This may be done immediately after the session or at the end of the semester when they have applied the concepts that have been taught.

Library Research Exercise

This group is researching an article about Madonna.

Step 1   What is Madonna's full name?

_____

Step 2   What source(s) did you use to find the name?

Title:_____

_____

Title:_____

_____

Step 3   What other source(s) could you use to find it?

Title:_____

_____

Title:_____

_____

Library Research Exercise

This group is writing an article about a recent Supreme Court decision.

Find a list of the current members of the Supreme Court.

Step 1   List all the sources you used to find the answer:

Title:_____

_____

Title:_____

_____

Title:_____

_____

Title:_____

_____

Library Research Exercise

This group is researching an article about the O.J. Simpson trial.

Focus on the meaning of "beyond a reasonable doubt."

Step 1   Find a legal definition for the phrase "beyond a reasonable doubt." Write it on the spaces provided below.

_____

_____

_____

_____

Step 2   What source(s) did you use to get the definition? List the titles.

Title:_____

_____

Title:_____

_____

Library Research Exercise

This group is writing an article about Newt Gingrich.

As you were researching the article, you discovered that he formed the Conservative Opportunity Society. Find out more about this organization.

Step 1   In what year did Gingrich form the society?_____

Step 2   What is the purpose of the organization?_____

_____

_____

_____

Step 3   Name a publication that is issued by this group.

_____

_____

Step 4   Name the title(s) of the source(s) that you used to acquire this information.

     Title_____

     Title_____

     Title_____

     Title_____

Library Research Exercise

This group is writing an article about the Republican's Contract with America.

Find some background information and determine where you would locate it in the library.

Step 1   What source(s) did you use to locate the information?

Title_____

_____

Title_____

_____

Title_____

_____

Title_____

_____

Finding Reference Sources in Mass Communications

How do I find an overview to materials in Mass Communications?
Journalism: A Guide to the Reference Literature
The Journalist's Bookshelf

Where can I find a dictionary for Mass Communications?
Words On Words: A Dictionary for Writers
NTC's Mass Media Dictionary

Where can I find biographical information:
Biography and Genealogy Master Index (print and CD-ROM versions)
Who's Who in America
Who's Who in Entertainment

How do I find addresses of organizations, associations, etc.?
Congressional Directory
Encyclopedia of Associations
Gale Directory of Publications and Broadcast Media
Literary Marketplace (LMP)
The United States Government Manual
Writer's Market
Also, consult the phone book collection

How do I find statistical information?
Statistical Abstract of (state)
Statistical Abstract of the United States

How do I find factual information for a story?
Facts on File
Editor & Publisher
Guinness Book of World Records
World Almanac
Also try CD-ROM databases such as:
- *Readers' Guide*
- *National Newspaper Index*
- *Social Sciences Index*
- *Westlaw*

How do I find dictionaries to confirm the spelling of words for different subjects?
Use the outline of the Library of Congress classification system and search the reference shelves.
Many disciplines have their own specialized dictionaries.

How do I locate style manuals for Mass Communications?
Los Angeles Times Stylebook
The Associated Press Stylebook
UPI Stylebook

Where are the books that might help me improve my writing?
The Magazine Article: How to Think It...
The Best American Sports Writing
The Sports Writing Handbook
Air Words: Writing for Broadcast News
Basic TV Reporting
Pulitzer Prizes

What are the names of a few journalism periodicals?
Columbia Journalism Review
Journalism Quarterly
The Quill

NOTES:

Activities for Individuals

This section contains:

Research? What Is It Exactly?
Gretchen McCord Hoffmann

Evaluating Resources
Dell M. Davis

Reading Citations: Is This a Journal Article or a Book or What?
Jeff Fadell

History Topics in Research Writing
Marilyn P. Whitmore

Public Speaking; Instruction for Multiple Sections of a Class
Mary Strow

Social Welfare Policy; Teaching How to Research a Policy
Cathy Seitz Whitaker

NOTES:

Research? What Exactly Is It?

GRETCHEN MCCORD HOFFMANN
Coordinator of Library Instruction
UNIVERSITY OF HOUSTON

Circumstances for the Instruction Session:

The English Department at the University of Houston (UH) is an adamant supporter of library instruction and has sought various ways to address this need in their curriculum, especially for their freshmen. All freshmen are required to take two semesters of composition in the English Department. In the past, it was thought that there were too many freshmen in these classes for the library to accommodate in classes; there are approximately 2,300 students each year (fall, spring, and summer semesters). A self-paced workbook was developed about ten years ago to handle the large number of students.

When I arrived at UH in the fall of 1994, the workbook was very much a source-based tool. I headed a task force which completely rewrote the book in less than one year to make it much more concept oriented. Our goal was to create a textbook which would teach our students how to use any academic library, not just ours. As a result, we have had offers from two custom publishers to publish the book. We are currently working with Kendall-Hunt and hope to have them publish it in early 1997.

In Reference to Libraries is the title of the resulting book and consists of 15 chapters and four appendices which address various aspects of using the library. We designed the book with the idea that students could keep it to use as a reference tool throughout their college careers.

Thus, the exercise completed by the students is no longer a part of the book but is distributed separately. This consists of 33 multiple-choice questions which can be answered on a scantron; the Library Instruction Program is responsible for grading. Although we would much prefer more open-ended questions, it simply would not be possible for us to grade this type of assignment.

The English Department is currently redesigning the curriculum for their lower level classes and is looking at ways of creating library assignments which are more course-integrated. The Library Instruction Program is being included in this discussion.

The following three chapters are excerpts from the UH book titled *In Reference to Libraries*. "Reading Citations" is presented as a side box to the chapters about using printed and electronic indexes. "The Research Process" is an addendum. I have added to it the selection called "Evaluating resources," which is also a side box to the chapter on locating materials and thus appears separately from "The Research Process." There are references throughout "The Research Process" to other sections of the book; I have removed these references in the excerpt which is included in this book, *Empowering Students; Hands-on Library Instruction Activities*.

In Reference to Libraries was edited by Gretchen McCord Hoffmann. Co-editors and contributors were Dell Davis, Jeff Fadell, Andrea Bean Hough, April Moreno, and Jeanne Newlon. The excerpt "The Research Process: What Exactly Is Research/A Research Paper?" was written by Gretchen McCord Hoffmann. (In this book the chapter is entitled "Research? What Exactly Is It?") "Reading Citations: Is This a Journal Article or a Book or What?" was written by Jeff Fadell. "Evaluating Resources" was compiled by Dell Davis.

Note: (Hoffmann, Gretchen McCord, ed. *In Reference to Libraries*. Houston: University of Houston Libraries, 1995. Excerpts reprinted from pp. 52, 64, 86, and 93-97 by permission of the editor and publisher. All rights are reserved. Permission is granted for one time reproduction only; any subsequent reproductions require additional permission requests.)

Suggestions for use in other settings:

It is suggested that the chapters in this section be used as supplemental text to classroom instruction. "Research? What Exactly Is It?" and "Evaluating Resources" would be used most effectively together with classroom instruction. Students could then complete an outside assignment using these sections. "Reading Citations" could be used as a separate handout for students independently of any instruction.

A variation would be to distribute the handouts before the library instruction class so that students could review them before coming to the class. The handouts could be discussed and reviewed during a library instruction session.

Hands-on Activity:

The student activity utilizing the research process begins on the next page.

The Research Process

According to *Webster's New World Dictionary*, a process is "a continuing development involving many changes." (Victoria Neufeldt and David B. Guralnik, eds. *Webster's New World Dictionary of American English*, 3rd college edition. New York: Prentice Hall, 1994. p.1072).

This is certainly true of the research process. Although specific steps can be identified and are usually followed more or less in a particular order, it is not a strictly linear process.

When you do research in the library, most often in preparation for writing a "research paper," your research will focus on finding information which supports a specific idea, usually the thesis statement of your paper. As you progress in your research, you will continually refer back to your thesis statement to guide you, and you may revise or modify your thesis statement somewhat as you go along, based on the information you discover. Likewise, you will continually refer to your original research strategy, and, based on the information you find and any modifications of your thesis statement, you may also revise your research strategy periodically.

The seven major stages of the research process are described below.
When you use this section, however, remember that this is just a loose description of the process. It is not meant to be used as a set of instructions to be followed rigidly. The key to doing successful library research is to keep your purpose in mind, continually evaluate what you have done so far, and be flexible in refining your goal and your strategy.

Part 1: Choose and define your topic

Writing a research paper is more than simply collecting and summarizing already published material. You will be defending your own ideas as stated in your thesis statement concerning your topic.

Most research papers that you write in college will be for a specific class, so your topic will relate to the subject matter of that class. You should choose something that you are interested in as well, since you will be spending a good bit of time researching the topic.

If you are having trouble choosing a topic, you might browse through your textbooks for some ideas, review your class lectures, speak to your professor, confer with a librarian, or spend some time browsing through journals within that subject area.

For an example we can follow through the whole research process, we'll use violent television shows as a topic.

Part 2:   Preliminary focus

Once you have at least a general idea of what your topic will be, you should begin your research by getting some background information on your topic and compiling an overview. This will help you to decide precisely what to focus on and where to look for more in-depth information. In addition, this stage may help you decide on a thesis for your topic of interest.

Reference sources like encyclopedias, subject dictionaries, and any specialized material such as yearbooks on your topic are good places to get started on this stage. For our topic of violent television shows, we might want to look at reference material on the history and development of television and programming, such as the *Encyclopedia of Television.*

Part 3:   Focus your topic

To write a coherent paper, you will need to have a well focused topic for many reasons. If your topic is too broad, you will not be able to state and support a good thesis statement. In addition, there will be so much published about your topic that you will not be able to address the issue in a paper of limited length. A quick search of only one index of popular journals for a two-year period reveals over 300 citations concerning television violence. To make this a manageable topic, we need to concentrate on some particular aspect of violence on television.

On the other hand, if your topic is too narrow, too limited, there may not be enough written about it. For example, we probably would not find more than two or three articles—if any—on violence in one particular television show.

Another potential problem which makes it difficult to locate enough material is choosing a topic which is too recent. If your topic is a very current event, there may not have been enough time for anything to have been published, or if published, to have been indexed so that it is easy to identify.

Some questions to consider in focusing your topic include the following:

- **What subject areas or disciplines does your topic touch on?** For example, issues of violence on television relate to journalism, social values, psychological causes and effects, trends in criminology, and child rearing.

- **From what differing points of view could you approach this topic?** For example, television violence could be of concern to the television industry, advertisers, parents, organizations addressing freedom of speech, legislators, educators, and law enforcement professionals.

- **What time period does this topic fit into?** For example, television became common in the 1950's. Regulation of programming has been an issue ever since.

Use the preceding questions to help you formulate a more focused thesis and topic. For our example, we may decide to focus on the correlation between the amount of violence shown on television and crime rates in the last ten years for the United States as a whole.

Our thesis statement will be that there is a positive correlation between the two and that it is increased crime which causes more explicit violence to be shown on television. The first part of this thesis statement (violence on TV) can be proved or disproved. The second part (increased crime rates) cannot be proved; we must produce an intelligible argument for this hypothesis, present information which we believe supports our argument, and explain why or how the information supports it.

Part 4: Decide what type of information to use

Now that we have a focused topic and thesis statement, we can begin work on collecting information. To decide what kind of information you need, consider the following questions:

1. **What level of information do you want?**
   Are you looking for scholarly research reports, news stories, statistics, or editorials?

For example, for our topic we should be able to find many news stories and arguments about the relationship between television violence and crime rates, as well as some research reports about how television shows affect behavior and about how changes in society are reflected in popular media.

2. **How in-depth or broad should your information be?**
   Do you want a book which will give you a comprehensive history of your topic, a book that summarizes published information on your topic, or an article that covers one specific aspect of your topic in great detail?

For our thesis, we will probably want some of each.

3. **Do you need any specialized information?**

For example, for our topic we want statistics which will give us both crime rates and the number of violent shows on television over the last ten years. We might also want to view some specific shows on videotape or look for interviews with criminals.

Part 5: Develop a search strategy

Your search strategy is a specific plan for how you will search for the information you need. It includes selecting the sources you will need, identifying terminology, combining your terms, and analyzing the results of your search.

Note: In the book, *In Reference to Libraries*, this section refers the reader to a chapter that goes into much more detail about searching and that includes a "search strategy worksheet."

Part 6: Locate, read, and evaluate the information

Once you have located the material identified in your search,

- you need to read it,
- take notes on it, and
- review your results.

Does this information address your thesis statement? Does it meet all of your needs? See the accompanying list "Evaluating Resources" for more help in answering these questions.

Part 7: Revise, refine, synthesize

As you work on synthesizing the information you have collected into a paper which supports your thesis statement, you should continually evaluate how well the information meets your needs. At any step in this process, you may need to pause to revise either your topic, your thesis statement, or your search strategy. This can include narrowing or expanding any of these three, changing the point of view you use, selecting new terminology, or choosing a different type of material.

Remember that the research process is not a linear step-by-step journey. Each of the stages defined above influences the others. Therefore, you should be open to retracing your steps and altering your path when necessary.

Evaluating Resources

DELL M. DAVIS

Social Sciences Librarian
UNIVERSITY OF HOUSTON

Now that you've located your resources, you should evaluate them to determine if the information presented is in line with the objectives for your research. Consider the following criteria:

Relevance

Is the content of the item suitable for your research?
To determine this, examine the table of contents. This will give you a list of chapter titles and subdivisions. If a preface or introduction is available, read it. In a journal article or book chapter, usually the lead paragraph or abstract will give you enough information to determine if the item is relevant. Be sure to check the date of publication. Does it correlate with your research needs?

Reliability

Is the information presented accurate and dependable?
One way to help determine the reliability of a book is to use book reviews. Another is to compare the facts with other documents on the same topic to check supporting facts or data.

Credibility

What are the author's credentials? Is the author an expert in the field?
Biographical reference sources can often give you this information.

Validity

Know where the information is coming from. Is the work based on personal opinion, original research, laboratory experiments, or other documentation? From what sources were the facts gathered?

Perspective

Be watchful of author bias, especially when looking for objective accounts. Consider the author's cultural, political, social, and economic background.

Timeliness

Check the date of publication. Are you looking for contemporary materials (sources which originated near or at the time of an event, idea or phenomenon)? Are you looking for a current account of an historic event?

References

Look for bibliographies or original research as attachments or appendices. References often give you an opportunity to check item validity and are a possible avenue to additional resources.

Purpose

Why was the item written?
The purpose can range from dissemination of information about an important study or research project, to the insight of a specific group of people, to propaganda.

Intended Audience

Who is the target audience? Children, laypersons, scholars, professionals?
This is often reflected in the author's writing style. Is this appropriate for your purposes?

Reading Citations: Is This a Journal Article or a Book or What?

JEFF FADELL

Reference Librarian
UNIVERSITY OF HOUSTON

In many bibliographies and indexes, you will find three types of material cited:

- Journal articles
- Essays or chapters from books
- Books

This distinction becomes important when you are looking for material in the library. To see if the library owns the article or chapter you need, you will have to look up the title of the journal or book in which it has been published, not the title of the article or chapter itself.

If the title is followed by a number or a part of a year such as a season, a month, or a date, it is the title of a journal. If the title is followed by the name of a city, a publisher, and a year, it is the title of a book.

Printed Index Citations

In a printed index, a title "in quotation marks" or in **bold-faced print** is the title either of an article in a journal or of an essay or chapter from a book.

A title in *italics* or underlined is the title of either a book or a journal. Book titles also appear in **bold-faced print** in some indexes.

Journal article:
Peeples, Faith & Loeber, Rolf. "Do individual factors and neighborhood context explain ethnic differences in juvenile delinquency?" *Journal of Quantitative Criminology*, 1994 (Jun), Vol 10(2), 141–157.

Chapter from a book:
Magnusson, David; Klinteberg, Britt & Stattin, Hakan. "Juvenile and persistent offenders: Behavioral and physiological characteristics." *Adolescent problem behaviors: Issues and research.* Ketterlinus, Robert D. & Lamb, Michael E. (Eds). Lawrence Erlbaum Associates, Inc: Hillsdale, NJ, 1994. xii, pp. 81–91.

Book:
Ketterlinus, Robert D. & Lamb, Michael E. (Eds.). *Adolescent problem behaviors and research.* Lawrence Erlbaum Associates, Inc: Hillsdale, NJ, 1994, xii, 238 pp.

In an electronic index, each part of the record will be labeled with an abbreviation, such as

- "TI" for title,
- "JN" for journal, or
- "SO" for source.

Journal article:
TI: Do individual factors and neighborhood context explain ethnic differences in juvenile delinquency?
AU: Peeples, -Faith; Loeber, -Rolf
JN: Journal-of-Quantitative-Criminology; 1994 Jun Vol 10(2) 141–157
PY: 1994
IS: 07484518
LA: English

Chapter from a book:
TI: Juvenile and persistent offenders: Behavioral and physiological characteristics.
AU: Magnusson, -David; Klintberg, -Britt; Stattin, -Hakan
BK: Adolescent problem behaviors: Issues and research. (Robert D. Ketterlinus, Michael E. Lamb, Eds.), pp 81–91. Lawrence Erlbaum Associates, Inc, Hillsdale, NJ, US; xii, 238 pp.
PY: 1994
IS: 0-8058-1157-5 (Hardcover); 0-8058-1157-5 (paperback)
LA: English

Book:
TI: Adolescent problem behaviors: Issues and research.
AU: Ketterlinus, -Robert-D. (ED); Lamb, -Michael -E. (Ed)
PB: Lawrence Erlbaum Associates, Inc; Hillsdale, NJ, US; xii, 238 pp.
PY: 1994
IS: 0-8058-1156-7 (hardcover); 0-8058-1157-5 (paperback)
LA: English

History Topics in Research Writing

MARILYN P. WHITMORE

Editor
LIBRARY INSTRUCTIONS PUBLICATIONS

Circumstances for the Instruction:

Several instructors who teach Research Writing in the English Department at the University of Pittsburgh have arranged with the Office of Library Instruction to teach six 50-minute library instruction classes near the beginning of the term. This timing provides a solid foundation for the students to become efficient information seekers and managers as they embark upon the class project .

During the course of the semester, each student writes a 25–30 page research paper on a topic of choice. Some topic modifications result when sufficient sources are not available locally.

The enrollment in each class is limited to 22 students. Three or four librarians typically provide the instruction, each on one of the specialized topics described in the section called Components of the Library Instruction. It is good for the students to have various presenters in the six sessions because of differences in style, voice, and knowledge base. Students like variety.

Objectives of the Instruction:

- Students will focus and analyze their topics.

- Students will develop a logical search strategy.

- Students will construct a list of keywords and concepts to elicit meaningful resources.

- Students will search the on-line catalog efficiently.

- Students will discern which periodical indexes or abstracts to search.

- Students will use government publications.

- Students will engage in a hands-on library search activity.

Components of the Library Instruction:

Class 1 content:

- Begin with a get-acquainted activity.

- Review the objectives and expectations of all six classes.

- Devote the first lecture to focusing and analyzing a research question; *Learning the Library* is an excellent resource text.

- Request that students turn in their approved research topics to the library instructor at the second class period.

Class 2 content:

- Utilize this class discussing search strategy and why one is so important.

- Include active learning elements to make this topic more interesting.

Class 3 content:

- Discuss the components of the on-line catalog.

- Spend time with the concept of Boolean searching.

- Include the use of official subject headings.

- Consume a major portion of the class time doing hands-on work.

Class 4 content:

- Devote this class to strategies for locating articles in print and electronic resources.

- Utilize some show-and-tell here to make it real.

Class 5 content:

- A government documents specialist will discuss print and electronic access to documents.

- A short hands-on assignment with document resources is the homework assignment due at the next class.

Class 6 content:

- The sixth session is devoted to individualized hands-on activities based on the chosen research topics of the students. Both the librarian and the instructor should be available for consultation during the whole session while the students are working in the reference area.

- Generally, each student must complete the activity during the library class time. Sometimes, however, they are retained by the students while their research papers are being written. At some point the activities must be turned in to the instructor; a few instructors have students report on the experience and discuss the tools during a class.

Hands-on Activities:

A selection of student activities of an historical nature is included in this chapter. Topics in other disciplines will be included in a forthcoming book from Library Instruction Publications.

It is extremely time consuming for the library instruction librarian to develop individualized search strategies for the student research topics but the English faculty report that the final papers show the value of the effort. When the student topics are given to the librarian at the beginning of the second class, it is possible to have the completed activities ready for the sixth class.

Evaluation:

A formal evaluation questionnaire has been developed and administered quite consistently for this series of library instruction presentations. The questionnaires are sent to the faculty member near the end of the term when the final papers are due and the students complete them. This timing is good because students will have had time to utilize the information gleaned in the six classes which includes the search strategy activity.

One question is set up listing the six classes and students are asked to respond on a scale of one to five as to the value of each class.

Several years ago, a pre-test was sent to several research writing classes about two weeks before the library presentations began. I personally believe it is useful to discover how much or how little the students know about using a library. The content of the library instruction classes can reflect the results of the pre-test findings. The content of the pre-test is included on the following page for the benefit of other librarians; it is not in the format or font used for student distribution.

An excellent source of information on evaluation is the publication issued by the Research Committee of the Library Instruction Round Table entitled, *Evaluating Library Instruction: Sample Questions, Forms and Strategies for Practical Use* (1995).

1. Did you have library instruction in high school? Yes___No___
2. Have you ever worked in a library? Yes___No___
3. Have you had a tour of this library? Yes___No___
4. When you search for books in a library catalog, do you most commonly
    a. search by known author or title?
    b. search by subject to locate authors and titles?
5. What is (name of on-line catalog)? Have you tried it? Yes___No___
6. What is InfoTrac (or other general title)? Have you tried it? Yes___No___
7. What is a SuDoc number?
8. List two reasons to use periodical articles for general reading, library assignments, research and term papers.
9. There are two basic types of periodicals; each has a different style of writing.
    a) Popular periodicals written in a non-scholarly style, often profusely illustrated, are usually called_____.
    b) Professional periodicals written by and for members of a profession are usually called _____.
10. What added piece of information do you find in an abstract that you do not find in an index?
11. What source must you consult to find out if this library has a periodical title?
12. Reference books are designed by arrangement and treatment to be consulted for authoritative information. They are not written to be read from beginning to end. Name three different categories of reference books.
13. A bibliography is:
    a. a book about the life of a person.
    b. a list of sources consulted.
    c. the place of publication and publisher of a book.
14. What would you get from a database or CD-ROM search?
    Have you tried any of these yet? Yes___No___
15. Using a scale of 1 (strongly agree) to 5 (strongly disagree), please answer the following:
    a)_____The library is important to my college education.
    b)_____My professors will expect me to be able to effectively use the library.
    c)_____Knowing how to use the library will help me in many of my courses.
    d)_____The library is important for life-long learning.
16. In what order do you consult the following when you are beginning a research project?
    (number from 1–5)
    _____periodical articles
    _____on-line and/or card catalog
    _____periodical indexes
    _____encyclopedias and dictionaries
    _____other libraries

Topic Investigation

Women in the military.

Investigate how historic exclusion and reserve combat exclusion has affected the women who choose the occupation.

Want to save time? Promise yourself to keep a record of your search strategy. Efficiency in your library work can be achieved when you **keep a log book** and write down every step you take, every subject you search, every reference source you search. By doing this, you will not have to retrace your steps because you will always know what you have already done.

CHECKLIST

log book	general periodical index
background information	index to public affairs periodicals
keywords	on-line catalog

Step 1   A really useful step is to read **background information** on this current and controversial topic. The following titles look very promising:

Women in the Military, by Carol Wekesser and Matthew Polesetsky (1991)
Women in the Military: an Unfinished Revolution, by Jeanne Holm (1992)

Step 2   Now you are ready to begin constructing a list of relevant terms, **keywords**, or concepts which you believe describe facets of this topic. They are essential before you begin delving into periodical literature.

_____   _____

_____   _____

_____   _____

Revise and/or add to the list as you proceed.

Step 3   Search a **general periodical index** to locate articles which have a popular or mass-audience point of view. Again, use the keywords from your list.

Periodical Abstracts and *Expanded Academic Index* are two general periodical indexes in electronic format; each provides access to more than a thousand "high demand" magazines and journals. Coverage begins about the mid–1980s and you can expect to find some articles on almost any topic you choose.

If your library doesn't have access to an electronic title, use *Readers' Guide to Periodical Literature*. This title indexes articles in about 200 magazines which are popular in nature. Also, use the *Readers' Guide* for earlier coverage when you need information published before the mid–1980s.

Step 4   Another periodical index which you may find useful for this topic is *PAIS* which stands for *Public Affairs International Service*. It covers periodicals, books, and international government documents in the fields of economics, **public affairs**, government policy, etc. The electronic version covers the 1970s to the present time.

Ask a librarian where you can locate this title. Then search *PAIS* using the same terms which you used in the earlier Steps. Some modification may be necessary because each discipline has its own vocabulary.

Step 5   Search the library's **on-line catalog** for books on your topic. An advantage of searching a machine-readable catalog is the ease with which it is possible to revise or change search strategies. Terms can be linked, combined, or excluded to match your search request.

Topic Investigation

The American worker and the industrialization of the United States.

Focus on the transition and its effects.

Want to save time? Promise yourself to keep a record of your search strategy. Efficiency in your library work can be achieved when you **keep a log book** and write down every step you take, every subject you search, every reference source you search. By doing this, you will not have to retrace your steps because you will always know what you have already done.

CHECKLIST

log book	on-line catalog
background information	index to public affairs periodicals
keywords	general periodical index

Step 1 Read some **background information** on this broad topic and begin to decide exactly what the focus will be. Two suggestions are listed below.

Working for Democracy: American Workers from the Revolution to the Present, by Paul Buhle and Alan Dawley (1985)

In the Shadow of the Statue of Liberty: Immigrants, Workers, and Citizens in the American *Republic, 1880–1920*, by Marianne Debouzy (1992)

Step 2 Now begin your project by constructing a list of relevant terms, **keywords**, or concepts which you believe describe facets of this topic. They are essential before you begin delving into periodical literature. Revise and/or add to the list as you proceed.

_____   _____

_____   _____

Step 3   Search the library's **on-line catalog** for additional book titles. An advantage of searching a machine-readable catalog or database is the ease with which it is possible to revise or change search strategies. Terms can be linked, combined, or excluded to match your search request.

Print the call numbers of any titles which you want to examine; if a printer is not available write them in your notebook.

Step 4   **Subject searching in the on-line catalog** can sometimes retrieve books which you could not find by keyword searching . The reason is because computers don't think, they simply match words. You get **only** the hits which include the exact keywords.

Look under the subject: working class—united states—history

Step 5   Search for periodical articles. An index which you will find useful for this topic is *PAIS* which stands for *Public Affairs International Service*. It covers periodicals, books, and international government documents in the fields of economics, **public affairs**, government policy, etc. The electronic version covers the 1970s to the present time.

Ask a librarian where you can locate this title. Then search *PAIS* using the same terms which you used in the earlier Steps. Some modification may be necessary because each discipline has its own vocabulary.

Step 6   Search a **general periodical index** to locate articles which have a popular or mass-audience point of view. Again, use the keywords from your list.

Periodical Abstracts and *Expanded Academic Index* are two general periodical indexes in electronic format; each provides access to more than a thousand "high demand" magazines and journals. Coverage begins about the mid–1980s and you can expect to find some articles on almost any topic you choose.

If your library doesn't have access to an electronic title, use *Readers' Guide to Periodical Literature*. This title indexes articles in about 200 magazines which are popular in nature. Also, use the *Readers' Guide* for earlier coverage when you need information published before the mid–1980s.

Topic Investigation

The political aspects of Puerto Rico at the beginning of the 20th century.

Explore how its political status as a commonwealth of the US had an impact on its society and cultural development.

Want to save time? Promise yourself to keep a record of your search strategy. Efficiency in your library work can be achieved when you **keep a log book** and write down every step you take, every subject you search, every reference source you search. By doing this, you will not have to retrace your steps because you will always know what you have already done.

CHECKLIST

log book	on-line catalog
overview	index to articles in public affairs
keywords	index to government publications

Step 1   *The Political Status of Puerto Rico*, edited by Pamela Falk (1986) is a title you should locate and examine for an **overview** of the topic and as a source for bibliographical references.

Step 2   Construct a list of relevant terms, **keywords,** or concepts which you believe describe facets of this topic. They are essential before you begin delving into periodical literature.

_____   _____

_____   _____

_____   _____

_____   _____

Revise and/or add to the list as you proceed.

Step 3   Search the library's **on-line catalog** for any of the references you identified in the bibliography. You should also continue searching both by keyword and by using the subject heading you see listed at the end of the record.

An advantage of searching a machine-readable catalog or database is the ease with which it is possible to revise or change search strategies. Terms can be linked, combined or excluded to match your search request.

Print the call numbers of any titles which you want to examine; if a printer is not available write them in your notebook.

Step 4   Search for more scholarly periodical articles covering **public affairs** topics.

An index which you will find useful for this topic is *PAIS* which stands for *Public Affairs International Service*. It covers periodicals, books, and international government documents in the fields of economics, public affairs, government policy, etc. The electronic version covers the 1970s to the present time.

Ask a librarian where you can locate this title. Then search *PAIS* using the same terms which you used in the earlier Steps. Some modification may be necessary because each discipline has its own vocabulary.

Step 5   Search for **government documents**.

The US government is the largest publisher in the world and has issued scores of books and reports on most any topic. *The Monthly Catalog of US Government Publications* is the most comprehensive source to access US federal publications. It is available on CD-ROM covering the years since 1976.

Ask a member of the library staff where you can locate a CD-ROM version for this class activity.

Topic Investigation

The Knights Templar, the order of military monks that was founded at the end of the first crusade.

Want to save time? Promise yourself to keep a record of your search strategy. Efficiency in your library work can be achieved when you **keep a log book** and write down every step you take, every keyword you search, every reference source you search. By doing this, you will not have to retrace your steps because you will always know what you have already done.

CHECKLIST

log book	on-line-catalog
background information	indexes and abstracts
keywords	bibliographies

Step 1   Search one of the general encyclopedias for **background information**.

Authoritative encyclopedias such as the *Encyclopedia Americana* and *Encyclopaedia Britannica* provide essays on aspects of most every topic. At the end of longer essays, select bibliographies will be included which can be used as a working list of sources for further searching. *Americana* has excellent essays on countries of the world.

Step 2   Search a specialized dictionary or encyclopedia.

A specialized work which you should search is called *Dictionary of the Middle Ages*, in 9 volumes (1982–1987). See v. 4, p.41–49. Locate this reference work and read the selection.

Step 3   Construct a list of relevant terms, **keywords**, or concepts which you believe describe facets of this topic; they are essential for further searching on this research project. Revise and/or add to these terms as you proceed.

_____   _____

_____   _____

_____   _____

Step 4   Search the **on-line catalog** for books. Look especially for *Murdered Magicians: The Templars and their Myths*, by Peter Partner (1982)

Step 5   **Which disciplines** will have been concerned enough to have written articles?

Can you think of any disciplines besides History which will have written on the Crusades?

DISCIPLINE   INDEXES or ABSTRACTS

_____   _____

_____   _____

Using your keywords and concepts, search the periodical indexes and abstracts Historical Abstracts covers the literature of history of the world.

Step 6   Search a **general periodical index** to locate articles which have a popular or mass-audience point of view. Again, use the keywords from your list.

Periodical Abstracts and *Expanded Academic Index* are two general periodical indexes in electronic format; each provides access to more than a thousand "high demand" magazines and journals. Coverage begins about the mid–1980s and you can expect to find some articles on almost any topic you choose.

If your library doesn't have access to an electronic title, use *Readers' Guide to Periodical Literature*. This title indexes articles in about 200 magazines which are popular in nature. Also, use the *Readers' Guide* for earlier coverage when you need information published before the mid–1980s.

Step 7   Need more references? Search for a **ready-made bibliography**.

Search *Bibliographic Index*. Every listing you identify in this index will have no less than 50 items included.

Topic Investigation

Children of European immigrants.

Focus on the difficulties they encountered as they tried to assimilate into the U.S. culture.

Want to save time? Promise yourself to keep a record of your search strategy. Efficiency in your library work can be achieved when you **keep a log book** and write down every step you take, every keyword you search, every reference source you search. By doing this, you will not have to retrace your steps because you will always know what you have already done.

CHECKLIST

log book	on-line catalog
overview and bibliographies	general periodicals
keywords	history periodicals

Step 1   An **overview** of the topic immigration can be found in the following two titles:

Harvard Encyclopedia of American Ethnic Groups (1980) p. 476-508.

Multiculturalism in the United States; A Comparative Guide to Acculturation and Ethnicity (1992). See the sections about the European groups.

Step 2   Examine the bibliographies carefully which are included at the end of the sections in the *Harvard Encyclopedia*. Copy the full information for titles which seem to have promise because you will want to locate them later.

Step 3   Construct a list of relevant terms, **keywords**, and concepts which you believe describe facets of this topic; they are essential for further searching on this research project. You may discover that it will be necessary to search for specific countries and regions which are included in the concept Europe. Keep that in mind as you construct and revise your list.

_____   _____

_____   _____

_____   _____

Step 4 Using these keywords, conduct a search in the library's **on-line catalog** to see what books have been published on the subject.

Look at the subject headings used for the titles you retrieve in the keyword search. Some of these may give you hints for further researching your topic. Try these:

> s=europe—emigration and immigration
> s=immigrants—united states
> s=european americans

Step 5 Search a **general periodical index** to locate articles which have a more popular or mass-audience point of view. Use the keywords from your list.

Periodical Abstracts and *Expanded Academic Index* are two general periodical indexes in electronic format; each provides access to more than a thousand "high demand" magazines and journals. Coverage begins about the mid–1980s and you can expect to find some articles on almost any topic you choose.

If your library doesn't have access to an electronic title, use *Readers' Guide to Periodical Literature*. This title indexes articles in about 200 magazines which are popular in nature. Also, use the *Readers' Guide* for earlier coverage when you need information published before the mid–1980s.

Keep your eye open for book reviews in this index. These can lead you to new books on the particular topic.

Step 6 Search for references which have appeared in the literature published in the field of **history**.

America: History and Life covers the history of the United States and Canada. It abstracts relevant articles, books, dissertations, and includes an index to book reviews. It is available in paper volumes from 1964 and on CD-ROM from 1982. Ask a librarian if the electronic version is available.

STUDENT(S)..

Topic Investigation

The Fourth Crusade 1202-1204

Focus on the political and religious motivations which brought it to an end.

Want to save time? Promise yourself to keep a record of your search strategy. Efficiency in your library work can be achieved when you **keep a log book** and write down every step you take, every keyword you search, every reference source you search. By doing this, you will not have to retrace your steps because you will always know what you have already done.

CHECKLIST
log book   bibliography
keywords & subject headings   index to articles in religion
on-line catalog   index to articles in history

Step 1   Construct a list of relevant terms, **keywords**, or concepts which you believe describe facets of this topic. They are essential to know before you begin searching. Revise them as you proceed.

_____   _____

_____   _____

_____   _____

_____   _____

Step 2   Locate the *Library of Congress List of Subject Headings* and determine how your keywords translate into official **subject headings** which will have been used in the on-line catalog. Here are a few; you add to that list.

Innocent III Pope
Crusades--Fourth 120201204
Schism--Eastern and Western Church

_____   _____

_____   _____

Step 3   Search the library's **on-line catalog** for books using the subject headings and keywords. An advantage of searching a machine-readable catalog is the ease with which it is possible to revise or change search strategies. With keyword, terms can be linked, combined, or excluded to match your search request.

Sir Steven Runciman is considered the most eminent writer on the crusades. Be sure you search the on-line catalog for his writings. Use the author search approach.

Step 4   A **ready-made bibliography** can be a big aid in the search process. Look in the catalog especially for *The Crusade: Historiography and Bibliography*, by A.S. Atiya (1962).

Step 5   Search for articles in the literature of **religion**.

The *Religion Index* provides access to the literature published in religion and theology since the middle 1970s. This index is now available in electron form as well as the print volumes. Ask a librarian if the CD version is in the library.

Step 6   Search for articles in the literature of **history**.

Historical Abstracts includes references to articles, books, and dissertations on the history of the world which have appeared in more than 2100 journals in about 40 languages. From 1982 to the present, Historical Abstracts is available on CD-ROM; earlier volumes must be searched in the paper version. Ask if the CD version is in the library.

Topic Investigation

The Feelings of the Germans on Anti-Semitic propaganda during the 1930s.

Did the German people know of Hitler's plan to eliminate the Jews?

Want to save time? Promise yourself to keep a record of your search strategy. Efficiency in your library work can be achieved when you **keep a log book** and write down every step you take, every subject you search, every reference source you search. By doing this, you will not have to retrace your steps because you will always know what you have already done.

CHECKLIST

log book	on-line catalog
disciplines	index to articles in history
keywords	tables of contents

Step 1   Speculate about **disciplines interested** to write about this topic. Then determine and list the name of the index or abstract which covers the periodical literature of that discipline.

DISCIPLINE   INDEX or ABSTRACT

_____   _____

_____   _____

Step 2   Construct a list of relevant terms, **keywords**, or concepts which you believe describe facets of this topic. They are essential before you begin delving into periodical literature. You add to this short list which follows.

national consciousness   national socialism

anti semitic or antisemiticism   psycho history

_____ _____

_____ _____

_____ _____

Revise and/or add to the list as you proceed.

Step 3   Search the library's **on-line catalog** with the keywords listed above. Look carefully at the subject headings that have been used and then search by subject using those exact headings. If you have any questions about subject searching, consult a library staff member.

One title which you should examine is *Germany Possessed*, by H.G. Baynes (1941). It is a psychological analysis of Hitler and the German people. Locate the call number by executing an author or title search.

Step 4   Search for articles in **history journals**.

Historical Abstracts includes references to articles, books, and dissertations on the history of the world which have appeared in more than 2100 journals in about 40 languages. From 1982 to the present, *Historical Abstracts* is available on CD-ROM; earlier volumes must be searched in the paper version.

Step 5   Search for articles in the indexes you identified in Step 1.

Step 6   Need additional references? Another electronic database to search is *Current Contents*.

Current Contents includes the **tables of contents of about 6,000 journals** in most academic fields for the past two years. Choose the section which will include history Then search for your keywords and examine the titles of the articles which are shown on the screen. Not all of these journals will be available here on campus but it is a good place to identify articles.

Topic Investigation

The Theories about the Japanese Bombing of Pearl Harbor.

Concentrate on the beginning of U.S. involvement in World War II.

Want to save time? Promise yourself to keep a record of your search strategy. Efficiency in your library work can be achieved when you **keep a log book** and write down every step you take, every subject you search, every reference source you search. By doing this, you will not have to retrace your steps because you will always know what you have already done.

CHECKLIST

log book	index to history periodicals
keywords	index to public affairs periodicals
on-line catalog	index to government publications

Step 1   Begin your project by constructing a list of relevant terms, **keywords**, or concepts which you believe describe facets of this topic. They are essential before you begin delving into periodical literature. Revise and/or add to the list as you proceed.

_____   _____

_____   _____

_____   _____

_____   _____

Step 2   Search the library's **on-line catalog** for books relating to this subject. An advantage of searching a machine-readable catalog is the ease with which it is possible to revise or change search strategies. Terms can be linked, combined, or excluded to match your search request.

Examine the subject headings that have been used and then search by subject using those exact headings. If you have any questions about subject searching, consult a library staff member.

Another really efficient practice is to examine the catalog entries carefully because there may be references to bibliographies. These will be useful to lead you another Step in the research process.

Step 3   Search for **articles in history and public affairs**.

America History & Life includes references to articles, books, and dissertations on the history of the United States and Canada. From 1982 to the present it is available on CD-ROM; earlier volumes must be searched in the paper version.

PAIS , which stands for *Public Affairs International Service*, covers periodicals, books, and international government documents in the field of public affairs, economics, government policy, etc. The electronic version covers the 1970s to the present time.

Step 4   Search for **government publications.**

The US government is the largest publisher in the world and has issued scores of books and reports on most any topic. *The Monthly Catalog of US Government Publications* is the most comprehensive source to access US federal publications. It is available on CD-ROM covering the years since 1976. Ask a member of the library staff where you can locate a CD-ROM version for this class activity.

Topic Investigation

The Liberation of the Republic of Ireland.

Focus only on the events occurring shortly before and after the Easter Sunday Revolution.

Want to save time? Promise yourself to keep a record of your search strategy. Efficiency in your library work can be achieved when you **keep a log book** and write down every step you take, every subject you search, every reference source you search. By doing this, you will not have to retrace your steps because you will always know what you have already done.

CHECKLIST

log book	index to history periodicals
background information	on-line catalog
keywords	tables of contents

Step 1   Read **background information** on your topic in order to grasp the topic in a framework, to identify the correct time period, and to identify keywords which will be essential for your research.

Authoritative encyclopedias such and the *Encyclopedia Americana* and *Encyclopaedia Britannica* provide essays on aspects of most every topic. At the end of longer essays, select bibliographies will be included which can be used as a working list of sources for further searching. *Americana* has excellent essays on countries of the world.

Step 2   Now you are ready to begin constructing a list of relevant terms, **keywords**, or concepts which you believe describe facets of this topic. Revise and/or add to the list as you proceed.

_____   _____

_____   _____

_____ _____

_____ _____

Step 3   Search the library's **on-line catalog** for books relating to this subject. An advantage of searching a machine-readable catalog is the ease with which it is possible to revise or change search strategies. Terms can be linked, combined, or excluded to match your search request.

Examine the subject headings that have been used and then search by subject using those exact headings. If you have any questions about subject searching, consult a library staff member.

Step 4   Search for articles in **history journals**.

Historical Abstracts includes references to articles, books, and dissertations on the history of the world which have appeared in more than 2100 journals in about 40 languages. From 1982 to the present, _Historical Abstracts_ is available on CD-ROM; earlier volumes must be searched in the paper version.

Step 5   Another periodical index which you may find useful for this topic is _PAIS_ which stands for _Public Affairs International Service_. It covers periodicals, books, and international government documents in the fields of economics, **public affairs**, government policy, etc. The electronic version covers the 1970s to the present time.

Ask a librarian where you can locate this title. Then search _PAIS_ using the same terms which you used in the earlier Steps. Some modification may be necessary because each discipline has its own vocabulary.

Step 6   Need more references? An electronic database to search is _Current Contents_.

Current Contents includes the **tables of contents of about 6,000 journals** in most academic fields for the past two years. Choose the section which will include history and political science. Then search for your keywords and examine the titles of the articles which are shown on the screen. Not all of these journals will be available on campus but it is a good place to identify articles.

Public Speaking; Instruction for Multiple Sections of a Class

MARY STROW

Librarian for Reference Services, Undergraduate Library Services
INDIANA UNIVERSITY, BLOOMINGTON

Circumstances for the Instruction Session:

Public Speaking is taught each semester to more than 1400 students enrolled in over 50 individual sections at the University of Indiana, Bloomington. Library instruction sessions are presented to all of these sections in the short span of three days. Students are required to research and present at least five short speeches; the first of these is due soon after the library session. Class length is 50 minutes and the number of students attending each library session ranges from 26 to 78. In past semesters, the students have attended sessions during the regular class period; more recently students sign up for mandatory sessions offered at a variety of times.

The library component of Public Speaking began as a response to an assignment in which students were asked to look at ten journal indexes and find one item from each on their topics. More an exercise in frustration than awareness, the assignment was impossible for many students to complete since topics were varied and indexes were specialized.

The library class session and accompanying homework assignment were developed collaboratively among librarians and the coordinator of the Public Speaking program. As personnel and technology have changed, modifications have been made. The combination of a session in the library followed by a research assignment has remained stable through the years the program has been in place.

Objectives of the Instruction:

Instructors as well as librarians have set three goals for the library instruction sessions:

1. To introduce students, mostly freshmen, to the Libraries and library resources;

2. To assure that students know how to focus/analyze a research topic; and

3. To provide students with a guided experience in identifying, locating, using, and evaluating a variety of information resources which they will consult when preparing their speeches.

Components of the Instruction:

Introduction:

Two to three sections of Public Speaking are often combined in one large room. Since hands-on experience in the classroom is not an option for 75 plus students, various "ice-breaking" activities are employed in such a large setting. General questions which require group responses are asked:

- "How many freshmen are in this class?"

- "How many of you have been in the library already?"

- "How many of you have logged in to the library via the campus network?"

More specific questions follow:

- "Who can tell me which database to use when you want to find a book?"

- "What is the name of the libraries' network?"

The intent is to engage the class as a whole, then specific individuals. Throughout this time the librarian walks around the classroom, continually speaking. In past years, other types of questioning methods have been used:

A. A list of "Pre-Search" questions was projected on an overhead:
   - What is my topic?

   - What is the purpose of my speech?

   - What do I already know about my topic?

   - What questions do I want to answer in my speech?

B. A "Search Strategy Checklist" has also been projected. It included such points as:
   - Determine the type of information needed.

   - List the keywords or terms which describe your topic.

   - Select appropriate books and/or articles.

   - Evaluate information gathered.

Focus on the task to be accomplished:

The librarian zeros in on the purpose of the session, reminding students about their responsibilities during and after the class, and telling them what she intends to accomplish in the session. She stresses that students should have already purchased the Library Resource Packet from a local bookstore and brought it to class. It is critical for them to have the Library Packet since the homework exercise is located inside. A quick overview of the Library Resource Packet is made, asking students to follow while making notes and listening to the librarian point out highlights.

The Library Packet contains:

- a bibliography ("S121 Source List") of printed and electronic resources for Public Speaking students;
- a list of "Sources for Facts and Statistics," and
- the homework assignment.

The "S121 Source List" and "Sources for Facts and Statistics" are included at the end of the student activity in this chapter. However, most of the references to Indiana University have been deleted so that the lists will be more useful to librarians who wish to adapt the structure to their own library instruction needs.

Breaking up a topic into keywords:

Another question is directed to the class: Why do we need to break down a topic? One reason is that information is accessed through the use of words, and thus if one knows several words which describe what one wants and can then be combined in a database search, the information will likely be retrieved more quickly and the results will be more relevant. This dialogue leads directly into an explanation of Boolean operators. A sample topic, volunteered by a student, is broken down by the librarian to illustrate how terms can be combined in the on-line catalog. For example, if the topic is recycling the librarian asks, "What are various aspects or sub-topics of recycling that we can investigate?" Sub-topics might be:

- types of materials—plastic, glass, metals;
- community involvement;
- educational/awareness programs.

The class has sometimes been split into groups during this segment and each asked to brainstorm about keywords on a topic.

Types of materials to be found:

The librarian demonstrates in class how to find five types of basic information in the libraries' on-line catalog and electronic periodical indexes. These are:

- a book,
- a magazine article/journal article,
- a newspaper article,
- a government document, and
- a fact or statistic.

The homework exercise mirrors the in-class demonstration by requiring students to find items on their topics in the same fashion, utilizing the library network. The exercise is to be completed within a week of the library lecture and turned in to the Public Speaking instructor for grading.

Evaluation

Critical review of materials is emphasized throughout the class. Students must be aware of the importance of this aspect, especially in light of the proliferation of electronic resources.

Evaluation of the library sessions has also taken place on several occasions. Surveys have been sent to instructors and resulting responses have fostered review and revision. In some years, librarians have attended instructor's year-end meetings to ask about the quality of resources used by students, ideas for improvement of the library sessions, and changes in the out-of-class exercise.

Suggestions for Teaching Variation

Librarians may use or adapt the teaching strategies which have been discussed in a number of ways, depending upon facilities, staffing, and budgets. We have frequently experimented, for example, with an in-class exercise as a way of involving students more actively. During a three-year period, we used presentation software in order to assure consistency in content when ten different librarians were teaching the sessions. We have also scaled down the number of sessions given during summer school and changed the sample topics often.

The key to planning, development, scheduling, and evaluation of a program of this magnitude is effective communication between the librarian and the Public Speaking Coordinator. As a result, both parties have thus far been able to design and continually improve the library sessions as course content and assignments change.

Public Speaking Library Exercise

Complete the following exercise outside of class and turn it in to your instructor. Items to turn in are the completed library assignment plus a photocopy or print-out for all those items indicated in this assignment.

Step 1   For your next speech, you will need to choose a topic, keeping in mind the purpose of the speech and its length. Your topic should be something of interest to you or something about which you would like to know more.

The topic of my next speech is: _____

_____

_____

Step 2   In order to find relevant library materials, you will need to think of several **keywords** or **subject headings** that describe your topic. Items may be listed under any or all of these.

Appropriate **keywords** or **subject headings** to use when searching for materials on my topic are:

_____

_____

Step 3   You will also need to determine the **categories of information** that you want to use to collect information for your speech. You must decide if you want:

- magazine articles?
- reference books?
- newspapers?
- government publications?

- primary sources?
- secondary sources?

List the categories:_____

_____

Step 4   A general fact or statistic is essential to a good speech. Many times you will
not need to find a statistic on your specific topic, but rather a general fact or
statistic which is related to your topic. For example, it would be difficult to
locate the number of accidental house fires in Bloomington, but a national
statistic on house fires would be easily located and just as effective in
conveying the frequency of the problem in a speech on home safety.

Referring to the bibliography in the Library Resource Packet entitled *Sources for
Facts and Statistics*, look for a fact or a statistic related to your topic. What did
you   find? Photocopy the page from the source you used and turn it in with this
exercise.   Be sure to write the name of the source on the photocopy.

_____

_____

_____

Step 5   Magazine and journal articles are found through periodical indexes and
abstracts. Consult the Source List included with this exercise and write below
the names of two indexes which would probably list articles on your topic.

Two appropriate indexes to consult for periodical articles on my topic are:

_____

_____

Step 6 Use the *Expanded Academic Index* or the *Business Index* to find two articles related to your topic Fill in the blanks below. Print a copy of the citations to turn in with this exercise. (NOTE: Avoid company profiles, annual reports, and book reviews.)

a) Title of one article from the *Expanded Academic Index* or the *Business Index*:

_____

_____

Author (if any): _____

Title of magazine or journal: _____

_____

Volume: _____ Date: _____ Pages: _____

Search by title in the on-line catalog to answer the next two questions:

Do the Libraries subscribe to this magazine or journal? _____

If so, where can it be found? _____

_____

b) Title of the second article from the *Expanded Academic Index* or the *Business Index*:

_____

_____

Author (if any): _____

Title of magazine or journal: _____

_____

Volume: _____ Date: _____ Pages: _____

Search by title in the on-line catalog to answer the next two questions:

Do the Libraries subscribe to this magazine or journal? _____

If so, where can it be found? _____

_____

Step 7   Newspapers are important sources for finding interviews, first-hand reports, speeches, and concise summaries of events.

Two sources for newspaper articles are:

National Newspaper Index
   This is a subject guide to articles that appear in the *New York Times, Washington Post, Wall Street Journal, Los Angeles Times*, and *Christian Science Monitor*.

NewsBank
   This title is a resource which provides access to the full texts of newspaper articles on microfiche.

Find **one** newspaper article from either one of these sources and print a copy of the citation. Turn in the printout with this exercise.

If you found your article on the *National Newspaper Index*, fill in the following blanks:

Title of article _____

_____

Author (if any): _____ Date: _____

Title of newspaper: _____

Section no. _____ Page no. _____ Column no. _____

If you found your article on *NewsBank*, fill in the following blanks:

Title of article (Headline) _____

_____

Author (if any): _____ Date: _____

Title of newspaper (Source): _____

Section no. _____ Page no. _____ Edition: _____

Step 8   IUCAT is Indiana University's computerized catalog for books, journals, media, and other material in the library system. Use IUCAT to locate a book on the Bloomington campus (BB) that is relevant to your speech topic. Print a copy of the citation and turn it in with this exercise.

Title of the book: _____

_____

Author: _____

Location: _____

Call number: _____

Step 9   One of your speeches may require the use of congressional testimonies which offer arguments for or against a controversial subject. U. S. Congressional Hearings provide not only testimonies, but also committee reports, descriptions, and/or discussions of social, economic health, education, and other current issues. Look over the Source List in the Resource Packet and identify an index which would help you find this kind of information.

Title of index: _____

Location: _____

Sources for Facts and Statistics

General Almanacs and Fact Books

World Almanac and Book of Facts. Annual

Information Please Almanac. Annual

Statesman's Yearbook. Annual

Europa World Yearbook. 2 vols. Annual

Famous First Facts.

The Almanac of American Politics. Annual
> Contains concise information on the President, Senators, Representatives, and governors, their records and election results, their states and districts.
> Factual information such as names and addresses of departments, services, and members of the federal government, descriptions of political parties, campaign finance figures, and statistics on each state.

S121 Source List

TO FIND ARTICLES FROM GENERAL OR POPULAR MAGAZINES USE:

Expanded Academic Index (InfoTrac) 1976–present
    Scope: Indexes journals in the areas of social sciences, humanities, and sciences. Includes both scholarly and general periodicals. Some items are available full text.

Public Affairs Information Services Bulletin (PAIS) 1915–
    Scope: A guide to current literature on political science, government, legislation, economics and sociology.

TO FIND ARTICLES FROM SPECIALIZED OR SCHOLARLY JOURNALS USE:

ABI/Inform 1976–
    Scope: A computer database which indexes journals in such fields as banking, economics, finance, insurance, public relations, and real estate.

Business Index 1985–
    Scope: Indexes journals in all areas of business, including economics and management.

ERIC 1966–
    Scope: An index to journal and report literature covering all areas of education.

TO FIND ARTICLES FROM NEWSPAPERS USE:

National Newspaper Index
    Scope: Indexes articles from the Christian Science Monitor, New York Times, Wall Street Journal, Los Angeles Times, and the Washington Post.

TO FIND GOVERNMENT PUBLICATIONS USE:

Government Documents Catalog Service (GDCS) 1976–
Monthly Catalog of the US Government Publications
>Scope: A current bibliography of publications issued by all branches of the federal government, including reports from Congress and the Bureau of Census Publications. The *Monthly Catalog* is available in both electronic and print formats.

CIS Congressional Masterfile 1970–
>Scope: An index to virtually all of the Congressional Committee Reports and Hearings of the US Government. Available in both electronic and print formats.

TO FIND BOOKS USE:

IUCAT
>Scope: IUCAT is the computerized catalog of the Indiana University Libraries. It provides access to most of the materials held at IU campuses throughout the state. Look for books, journals, media, and government publications by author, title, subject, or keyword.

Card Catalog
>Scope: While IUCAT contains all of the current records, the card catalog is valuable for finding books acquired by the IU-Bloomington campus prior to 1976.

Social Welfare Policy; Teaching How to Research a Policy

CATHY SEITZ WHITAKER
formerly Buhl Social Work Librarian
UNIVERSITY OF PITTSBURGH

Circumstances for the Instruction Session:

Many courses in the School of Social Work at the University of Pittsburgh require a paper in which the student researches social welfare policy. The student is asked to choose a topic and complete a paper in which some or all of the following aspects are addressed:

- background on the social problem;

- development of proposed policies to address the problem;

- how these policies are translated from proposed legislation into law;

- once enacted, how the new policies mandated by law are implemented, and

- an evaluation of whether the policy is successful and possible attempts to alter the policy.

The courses in which this type of assignment are used include undergraduate, Masters and PhD level classes. Dissertations are also written which follow this format.

If the instructor has asked the students to include all the aspects of the policy process as described above, this can be a very complicated and difficult assignment. Typically, the instructor will ask the librarian to teach the class for a one, two, or three-hour period to instruct the students in how to conduct the research for the papers. Classes may have many or few students depending on the level of the course.

Objectives of the Instruction:

There is usually a great deal of student apprehension about this assignment. The first objective is to reassure the students that it is manageable. This requires that the librarian assure students that, in addition to the class session, a librarian will be available to meet individually perhaps several times during the course of the student's research. Most students who produce a high-quality paper for this assignment cannot do so without individual help because of the very many library tools and techniques which they must use to cover the scope of the assignment. Librarians responsible for helping this group of students must be prepared for requests for extensive individual help. Students should be required to phone to make an appointment for individual library help. Make it clear from the beginning how this is to be arranged.

Ensure that all students have the knowledge about policy necessary to do the library research for the assignment. They must know what policy means and that policies are in place at agency, local, state, and federal levels. Students need to understand the basic steps in the policy-making process. If their assignment includes a legislative history of a law establishing policy, they must understand how a bill becomes law. These elements are covered in the outline on researching social welfare policy in the "Components of Library Instruction."

Most instructors will cover some or all of these points in their classroom lectures. When the library session is set up, the librarian can ask the instructor to make sure students are familiar with these substantive issues. Inevitably, some students will not yet have a grasp of all these topics before they come to the library instruction session, therefore, the librarian will have to do some basic instruction on policy entirely apart of library-related issues.

Review carefully the factors students should consider when choosing a topic. It is crucial that students pick an appropriate topic for this kind of assignment, and they often need help to understand why some topics will be very difficult or impossible to research. Policy at the city, county, or state level may not generate enough literature, especially the kind available in libraries, for the students to do sufficient research. Students will have to rely upon interviews and possibly documents obtained through personal contact.

Sometimes students want to research a policy at an agency where they have worked, and they must understand that they will have to procure most of the research material that they use themselves. If part of their assignment is to evaluate the effectiveness of the policy, then they must choose a policy that has been in force long enough for analysts to have written about the success. They must also avoid policies that are too broad in scope or so narrow that information is not available. The original *Social Security Act* is not a good choice!

Break down their research into manageable components and suggest the order in which they should do research, basically following the order of the policy-making process. This is outlined in the handout "Researching Social Welfare Policy at the Federal Level; a Basic Outline," which is the outline for the lecture portion of the class. Most students will not absorb the entire lecture, but with a copy of the handout they can get started and return for help when they get stuck.

Give students hands-on activities in order to learn library tools.

Encourage students to cope in part with their anxiety over the assignment by starting their research early!

Components of the Library Instruction:

The bulk of the class is conducted primarily in lecture form. The handout "Researching Social Welfare Policy" can be used as the lecture outline. The outline is in five parts.

Part I covers primarily substantive issues with which some students will be familiar. The librarian can ask the class instructor to review this in class with them. It is helpful to have the instructor make clear which parts of the policy process covered in Step 3 are to be included in the paper. In Step 4, the students can look at the sources listed as the librarian covers them. The *"Green Book"* is by far the most important.

Part II is an overview of basic library research in social welfare. Many social work students will have had a library session and experience with these materials.

Part III reviews government publications students must use if they are to cover how the policy was established in law.

Part IV provides details about how a policy moves through the process into a law.

Part V covers the last sequence of the students' research, which explores how their policy was implemented, how well it worked and whether and what changes were made to it. To complete this part, the students will use the same sources that are covered in Parts II, III, and IV plus possibly the *Monthly Catalog of Government Publications*.

Hands-on Activities for Students

Students should be given some practical hands-on activities to familiarize themselves with library sources and the search strategy to follow in order to conduct social welfare policy research.

If time remains during the library instruction session, students can examine the materials covered in the lecture. If students are not familiar with *Social Work Abstracts*, they should have the opportunity to use it under the librarian's supervision. A list of suggested topics may be helpful to students who have not yet chosen topics. More advanced students, who have done background research and have chosen a topic, can begin by looking in the government sources, although the class ususaly ends before they experience much success. Students may wish to make an appointment with the librarian at the end of the session.

Evaluation

Instructors and students are encouraged to provide feedback about the usefulness of the handout and the class session.

Researching Social Welfare Policy at the Federal Level; A Basic Outline

PART I   UNDERSTANDING POLICY

Step 1   What does "social policy" mean?

In general, policies are statements on a government's position on an issue. The field of social work has its own dictionaries and that is a good source to consult for a definition. The *Social Work Dictionary* (1991) defines social policy as:

The activities and principles of a society that guide the way it intervenes in and regulates relationships between individuals, groups, communities, and social institutions... Social policy includes plans and programs in education, health care, crime and corrections, economic security and social welfare made by governments, voluntary organizations, and the people in general.

Policies may:
- be purposely developed and written
- be a loose set of general principles not carefully defined
- be made by a private agency
- be made by a government (city, county, state, federal)
- include principles or goals
- include programs intended to meet goals of the policy

Step 2   What level of policy will you research?

In order to research policy, you must know the level at which it originated—agency, local, state, or federal. Government policy at the federal level is the focus of this guide because federal documents are widely distributed and easily accessible. Official publications from state and local jurisdictions are not widely distributed and therefore more difficult to locate. You may have to contact these directly. Discuss it with a librarian.

There are numerous examples of policy. The US government legislates policy by passing laws, just one example is the *Americans with Disabilities Act*. The National Association of Social Workers publishes a book which includes their policies called *Social Work Speaks*. Social agencies have policies which guide their operations and activities.

Step 3   Decide what aspects you want to research.

In order to research policy, you must decide what parts of the process you will examine. You must decide whether to focus on the policy itself (the principles and objectives that are debated and finally adopted) or the programs that are established to implement policy.

Policy is often viewed chronologically. The policy-making process has several steps. Joseph Hefferman lists six stages of the policy process in his book *Social Welfare Policy* (1991). They are:

1.   Definition
2.   Formulation
3.   Selection
4.   Implementation
5.   Evaluation
6.   Adjustment

The **Definition stage** occurs when people recognize that something must be done about a problem, their needs and goals are voiced.

The **Formulation stage** occurs when interested parties lobby to persuade the government to adopt the measures they prefer for addressing the problem.

The **Selection stage** usually occurs when legislation is passed, a policy is declared, and programs may be described.

The **Implementation stage** occurs when objectives and complex procedures are further specified by the development of administrative codes and put into action with social programs. Social workers must understand what the policy requires them to do.

The **Evaluation stage** occurs when evidence is collected on the failures and/or successes of the policy.

The **Adjustment stage** occurs when policies are changed.

Step 4   Choose the policy to research.

Keep in mind that a policy based on a law that was passed in the last two years may be difficult to research because fewer reports and articles will have been written. A policy that has been in existence for a long time, such as social security, will have volumes written and you will need to focus on a specific aspect.

Where do you begin looking for the policy you want to research? Browse the following titles for ideas.

1.   The best single source of information on government programs is the *Overview of Entitlement Programs...Green Book.* It covers background material and statistical data on government programs which are within the jurisdiction of the Committee on Ways and Means. Most federal social welfare programs are covered. A new edition comes out every year.

2.   *Federal Programs Affecting Children and Their Families* covers about 125 federal programs, each with a program description, reference to the law establishing the program, funding levels, and number of children participating in the program. This report of the House Select Committee on Children, Youth and Families is usually published every year.

3.   *Developments in Aging* is issued by the Senate Special Committee on Aging. Volume I is a detailed overview of federal programs for the aging and Volume II is a compilation of reports prepared by federal agencies describing their agency's programs for the aging.

4.   *Major Legislation of the Congress* provides brief summaries of legislative issues currently before Congress and lists and describes laws passed in those areas. It comes out twice a year with annual cumulations.

5.   *Congressional Quarterly Almanac* provides an annual summary of legislation in different areas including health and human services, education, housing and community development.

PART II   PRELIMINARY RESEARCH FOR BACKGROUND INFORMATION

Once you have chosen a policy area, you will need material from a variety of sources for your research. The best background information will be found in articles and books about the policy and the subject.

Step 1   Begin to construct a list of relevant terms, keywords, or concepts which you believe describes facets of this topic. They are essential before you begin delving into periodical literature.

Step 2   Search for articles on the subject/policy using the list of keywords. Periodical articles can be identified by searching indexes which may be either in paper volumes and/or available in electronic format such as CD-ROM.

A.   One of the most useful indexes for researching social welfare policy is *Social Work Research and Abstracts* in print and its electronic counterpart called *Social Work Abstracts Plus.*

B.   Another option is to search a general periodical index to locate articles which have a more popular or mass-audience point of view.

Periodical Abstracts and *Expanded Academic Index* are two general periodical indexes in electronic format; each provides access to more than a thousand "high demand" magazines and journals. Coverage begins about the mid–1980s and you can expect to find some articles on almost any topic you choose.

If the library doesn't have access to an electronic title, use *Readers' Guide to Periodical Literature.* This title indexes articles in about 200 magazines which are popular in nature. Also, use the *Readers' Guide* for earlier coverage when you need information published before the mid–1980s.

The indexes you use will depend on the policy you are researching.

Step 3   Search the library's on-line catalog for books which deal with the policy you are investigating. An advantage of searching a machine-readable catalog or database is the ease with which it is possible to revise or change search strategies. Terms can be linked, combined or excluded to match your search request.

When closely related or synonymous terms are linked with the "or" command, the chances of locating more titles is greater. Teens "or" Youth is an example.

When terms describing different concepts are tied together with the "and" command, the number of titles found is restricted. In other words, it narrows the search to those titles most relevant to the specific topic.

Since you are searching for books which discuss policy you might link the keyword "policy" with words which describe your topic. For example, link policy and deinstitutionalize.

By now the student will have learned about an issue and hopefully a particular policy or law that addresses it. Some of the best materials for continued research are documents issued by the federal government. Looking for these documents will be easier after having read background information in periodical articles and books. The appropriate public law may even have been identified..

Different types of government publications are produced at different stages of the policy process. Most government publications are generated in the policy formulation and selection stages as the bill becomes a law. The process, and the documents generated, usually follow the same pattern in the House and in the Senate. A bill must be approved by both chambers of Congress and by the President before it can become law. A brief outline of the process is listed below.

1. The bill is introduced in the full House or Senate and is immediately assigned to a committee.
    Documents generated are:
    a. *Congressional Record* (a daily periodical with the verbatim transcripts of what is said on the House and Senate floors, and a record of all votes)
    b. Bill (the form in which most legislation is introduced)

2. The committee usually refers the bill to a subcommittee for study, hearings, revisions, and approval.
    Documents generated are:
    a. Hearings (transcripts from experts, interested officials, and interest group representatives who come to testify for and against the bill. Hearings may also include prepared statements. They are an excellent source of information)
    b. Committee Prints (reports or studies prepared at the request of the committee to help it investigate a bill)

3. The subcommittee sends the bill back to the full committee, which may amend or rewrite the bill.
    Document generated:
    a. Committee Report (which may contain the bill itself, analysis of the bill, and recommended amendments)

4. The full committee decides whether to do nothing about the bill and thereby kill it or to send the bill to the floor of its chamber with its approval. If the Committee chooses to recommend passage of the bill it will issue a Committee Report.

5. The leaders of the chamber then schedules the bill for debate and vote.
   Document generated:
   a. *Congressional Record*

6. The bill is debated, amendments are offered and voted on, and a final vote is taken.
   Document generated:
   a. *Congressional Record*

7. If the bill is passed in different versions by the two chambers, a conference committee composed of members from each chamber works out the differences.
   Document generated:
   a. Conference Report
   The bill is returned to each chamber for a vote on the revised bill.
   Document generated:
   a. *Congressional Record*

8. Finally, the President can sign the bill making it law.
   Documents generated if the President does sign:
   a. The act will be first published individually as a Slip Law, later compiled into *Statutes at Large*, and finally codified in the *United States Code*
   b. Possibly it will be included in *Weekly Compilation of Presidential Documents* (a weekly publication with statements, messages, and press conferences of the President)

   The President may veto or refuse to sign the bill.
   Document generated if the President does not sign:
   a. *Weekly Compilation of Presidential Documents*

9. In the event of a Presidential veto, each chamber must approve the bill by at least a 2/3 majority to override the veto and make the bill into law.
   Document generated:
   a. *Congressional Record*

PART IV   IDENTIFYING DOCUMENTS GENERATED WHEN A POLICY BECOMES LAW

First you will probably want to find your policy as it was originally passed as law. The best tool for this is *Statutes at Large*. Then you will want to use an index to find the other government documents discussed above which were generated when your law went through the House and Senate as bills. The best tool for this is *CIS Index*.

When a law is first passed it is issued separately as a "slip law." Try to avoid researching laws that are so recent they are available only as slip laws because these laws are so new not much information will be available on them. New laws are later published together in *Statutes at Large*.

Step 1   Use *Statutes at Large* to find your policy as passed into law.

Statutes at Large contains the full-text of all laws as they are passed. Every two years the Senate and House begin a new Congress. Each Congress has two sessions; each session lasts one year and each volume of *Statutes at Large* covers one session of Congress.

As laws are passed, they are given a coded number starting with the number of the Congress, followed by a dash and a number that represents the number of that law's place in the sequence of laws enacted by that Congress. For instance, "100–123" would be the 123rd law passed in the 100th congress. Most of the laws you will research will be Public Laws. Their numbers will look like "PL 100–123." Once you learn the "PL" number for your law, write it down. You will use it later.

In *Statutes at Large*, the laws are arranged by law number and, therefore, chronologically by date passed. If you know the date your law passed, or the PL number, you can go to the appropriate year and look it up by date or law number. If you do not know the date or passage or the law number you will have to use the index. Each volume of the *Statutes* has an index that covers all the laws passed in the year, or session, that the volume covers. Laws are indexed by subject and title. If you do know the year that your law passed, or its public law number, you might want to check for background material in books or journals before starting your search in government documents.

Step 2   Use *CIS Index* to identify government documents generated when your policy became law.

CIS Index began publication in 1970 and cites federal publications that are generated in the legislative process. If you are researching the legislative history of a bill passed since 1970, it should be the only reference source you need to use to identify documents to review. If your law passed before 1970, you will need to search the *Monthly Catalog of Government Publications*.

Steps to locate bills that became law before 1983:

The paper version of the *CIS Index* is in two parts: (1) an Index volume, with abstract numbers which refer to abstracts containing citations and descriptions of documents, and (2) the Abstracts volume, where abstracts are arranged by their numbers. In the back of the Abstracts volume is a section called "Legislative

Histories." Find the section that covers the session of Congress in which your law was passed. Within that section, the laws are arranged numerically by public law number. *CIS Index* will give you the abstract numbers for documents pertaining to that law. Find your law.

Steps to locate bills that became law after 1983:

Since 1984, *CIS Index* has included a separate volume called "Legislative Histories." Look in the volume for the year that your law passed. Laws are arranged by PL number. Find your law.

Note: *Congressional Masterfile* (1970 to present) is the name of the electronic version of the *CIS Index*; ask if your library has this title. You will be able to do keyword and public law searching on this version.

PART V   RESEARCHING POLICY IMPLEMENTATION, EVALUATION, AND ADUSTMENT

To research how a policy or program was implemented and to find evaluations of its success, you can use books, journal articles, and government documents. To find books and journal articles, use the same sources described in Part II.

To find government documents, use *CIS Index* or the *Monthly Catalog of Government Publications*, in either the paper or electronic format. The *Monthly Catalog* is more comprehensive than *CIS Index* and, therefore, may include some material on your policy not included in *CIS Index*.

TOPICS

Students who haven't made a decision about which policy to research might select one of the ideas below to help them focus.

- Rebuilding the inner city and initiatives to address poverty
- Severely retarded people in America
- Current child and family policy in the US
- Homelessness and the shelter system
- Raised by the government, or America's child welfare system
- Options for children living apart from their natural families—homeless; abused; mentally retarded

- Child poverty and public policy
- Urban poverty and the American underclass
- Early childhood education
- Home schooling
- Transitional child care and the *Family Support Act*
- Domestic tyranny—family violence
- G.I. bill—educational and social benefits
- Services for infants and toddlers with disabilities
- A woman's legal right to abortion
- Facilitating the employment of people with disabilities
- Child abuse or maltreatment
- Education for handicapped children
- Foster child health care
- Legal drinking age
- Food banks and hunger as a national crisis
- Indian child welfare administration
- Legal guardianship and grandparents
- Parent child incest
- Legal immigrants and undocumented aliens

NOTES: